PRAISE FOR SAMIR'S
RESULTS FROM HI̲_ ̲ ̲ ̲...

"Guidance and mentorship, with a personal touch. This book is a must-read for leaders, young and old, who are looking to take their career to the next level. Learn how you can create a legacy, and the financial reward that should accompany it."
—Edward P. Larkin, PE,
LaBella Associates, Vice President

"*The Millionaire Exit* is a rare gem—a practical, heartfelt guide for entrepreneurs who are not just building businesses but building legacies. Samir Mokashi speaks directly to those who have poured their lives into their ventures and now face the emotional and strategic challenge of stepping away. His book offers not just theory but a real-world roadmap filled with lessons you won't easily find elsewhere. If you're a founder looking to exit on your terms—and walk away wealthy—this is the guide you've been waiting for."
—Ashok M. Kakade, P.E.,
Fellow of ACI, ICRI, & ASCE, Principal Engineer

"Samir's *The Millionaire Exit* isn't just a manual on selling a business; it's a deeply personal and honest reflection on the founder's journey. Having witnessed parts of that journey, I appreciated how openly he shares the lessons he learned and the emotional weight of walking away from something you've built. There's no sugarcoating here—just real insight, hard-earned wisdom, and practical tools for anyone looking to build, grow, and eventually exit a business on their terms."
—Ganesh Chapagain, CEO & Founder of Aoka

"As an immigrant who started at the bottom and worked my way to the C-suite, *The Millionaire Exit* spoke to me on every level. Samir Mokashi captures the mindset, grit, and strategic thinking it takes to build something from nothing—and then exit with wealth and purpose. This isn't theory. It's a practical, heartfelt guide from someone who's lived it. If you're building a business with the long game in mind, this book is your blueprint."

—Srinivasan Ranganathan,
Executive Vice President and Chief Financial Officer

"I found myself smiling at the simplicity and practicality of some lessons that are deceptively powerful and worth the million-dollar exit! The book encourages you to appreciate every step of the journey—and then monetize that journey in a way that leaves everyone winning. It's a celebration of courage, hustle, heart, and the dream of building something that matters."

—Milin Tipnis, Former CFO and Executive at IBM

"As Samir's sister, I've watched him build, bustle with creativity, and somehow stay optimistic, no matter how tough the problem is. Not surprisingly, *The Millionaire Exit* is equal parts business wisdom and big brother life lessons—minus the part when I used to roll my eyes as he generously advised me. It is honest, structured, and full of grounded wisdom. It's part memoir, part toolkit, and entirely actionable. The personal touch—sharing mistakes, growth pains, and emotional crossroads—gives the book real heart. It's not just about how to sell a business; it's about how to build one worth buying, while living a life worth remembering."

—Vaishali Mokashi, Senior VP Strategy and Planning

"This book is a must-read for aspiring entrepreneurs and seasoned business owners alike. With its straightforward, common-sense approach, it demystifies the process of creating, building, and ultimately exiting a business as a millionaire. The step-by-step guidance Samir provides is not only easy to understand and practical but also incredibly insightful, making successful implementation possible. Whether you are just starting out or have been in business for years, Samir's approach of focusing on 'The Exit Roadmap' will serve as a guide in helping you achieve financial independence and personal satisfaction through your business transition. A must-read for anyone serious about exiting their business as a millionaire!"

—Joseph Pinzone, AIA, LEED AP, NCARB,
Ex Managing Principal SERA Architects

"I've worked with Samir for over two decades, and he is a true success story. He takes a deeply personal approach to business development that strategically and methodically searches for the fundamentals of powerful client relationships."

—Alec Holser, FAIA, Founding Principal, Opsis
Architecture, Registered in Oregon and Idaho

"This is the inspiring journey of an immigrant entrepreneur who not only built a highly sellable business but also achieved an extraordinary exit. In this book, Samir shares his real-world experience and actionable insights to help any entrepreneur design a strategic exit plan and maximize the value of their business when it's time to sell."

—Chi Wong, DVP Operations,
Promotional Merchandise Agency

"I've had the privilege of knowing and working with Samir Mokashi since 1994, when we were both employees at a major consulting firm. Over the past 15 years, I've watched his journey closely and witnessed his remarkable growth as a business leader and visionary. *The Millionaire Exit* is a true game-changer—a master key that unlocks opportunities many business owners don't even realize exist. Samir offers invaluable insights on making your company truly irresistible to buyers, all while remaining grounded in your core values. This book goes beyond financial success; it's about building a lasting legacy, creating a positive impact in your community, achieving true freedom, and exiting on your terms with pride and purpose."

—Majid Habibi, Founder,
Managing Principal, MEC Engineering

"This is the kind of book that whispers, 'You can do this.' Each chapter feels like sitting down with a mentor who cuts through noise and hype, showing you exactly how to start strong, grow strategically, and leave with a smile—and a financial reward. I wish I had had this book 20 years ago when I co-founded a business."

—Alan Scott, FAIA, Director of Sustainability,
Building Science Solutions

GREETINGS AND WELCOME

This is a book about exiting as a millionaire.

The lessons shared here are applicable to all entrepreneurs wanting to know the secret to a six, seven, or eight-figure payout.

This is not a book about theory; it is based on a real-life story—my story. It is about starting with nothing and walking away wealthy.

I'll share the wisdom and lessons I've learned as an immigrant entrepreneur, moving from nothing to building generational wealth.

The good news is that you don't have to be extraordinary to be successful.

Instead, you get to bring a new mindset and smart approach to the ordinary things you do in your business every day.

Here's to that "little extra!"

Thank you for being here.

P.S.

Eighty percent of most small business owners' net worth is their business. Yet 70% don't know how to monetize. Avoid the pitfalls with *How To Know If You're Ready For Your Millionaire Exit* at mybizmc.com/book.

P.P.S.

A back story on the signature above. It is my name in Devanagari script in a calligraphy style. It is an ancient script used by Hindu scriptures, written thousands of years ago in Sanskrit. As an undergraduate architecture student, I experimented with Devanagari calligraphy to connect with my Indian heritage. The stroke of Devanagari script is opposite of the western calligraphy. I customized off the shell fountain pens to do this. Over time I became proficient, and this signature evolved. I use it to sign my sketches, my diaries, and books. It has three alphabet sounds, "sa," "mi," and "r." Devnagari script is phonetic; there are no silent words, and each word is pronounced consistently as written.

THE
MILLIONAIRE
EXIT

WALK AWAY WEALTHY BY BUILDING A
GREAT CULTURE AND MAKING AN IMPACT

A Proven Strategy for Leaders to Scale, Sell, and Leave a Legacy

Samir Mokashi, CEPA® M.Arch. Ar.

The Millionaire Exit
Walk Away Wealthy by Building a Great Culture and Making an Impact
A Proven Strategy for Leaders to Scale, Sell, and Leave a Legacy
Samir Mokashi CEPA® M.Arch. Ar.

www.TheMillionaireExit.com

Legal and Earnings Disclaimer

TABLE OF CONTENTS

FOREWORD

When Samir Mokashi asked me to write the foreword for his book, *The Millionaire Exit,* I was flattered but also caught off guard. I know and like Samir, but I'm not a fan of most business books. They are typically filled with buzzwords and cliches and have some sort of "program" they want you, the reader, to follow—a program that will solve all your problems.

However, then I got into *The Millionaire Exit,* and I quickly figured out that this book is different. It is *not* like most other business books and is—in one word—extremely practical. That's because it is written by someone who has actually done what he is telling you, the reader, to do.

Samir gets what entrepreneurship is all about—and what differentiates real entrepreneurs like him from people who are just small business owners. That is how to not just make a living from your business—even a good one—but how to build significant value that you can extract upon exit.

What you're about to read is a blueprint for changing lives, building wealth, making an impact, and leaving a legacy. It's not what pop culture portrays entrepreneurship to be—coming up with a new idea and then getting rich quickly by finding outside investors. Samir's approach—that he has laid out beautifully in this book—is what I like to call "getting rich slowly." It will work for anyone who is willing to take the leap and do the work.

That's the reason you'll want to read this book. Because if you're like most entrepreneurs—especially in the architecture, engineering, or construction world—you didn't start your business just to work more hours, make a modest income, and retire on social security (and fumes). You started it to create something meaningful, something valuable, and something that gives you options.

Samir is the real deal—an immigrant entrepreneur who started with nothing, except grit, vision, and the willingness to do every job (including cleaning toilets on the graveyard shift). He built a business that scaled, succeeded, and sold. And now, he's giving you the roadmap.

You'll discover:

- How to start smart, so you don't spend years undoing rookie mistakes
- How to grow strategically, with systems and people who support your vision
- How to prepare your business for sale—so it's not just valuable; it's irresistible to buyers
- How to move on—to your next venture, your next passion, your next life—with confidence, clarity, and cash in the bank

It's all in this book: *The Millionaire Exit.*

I write these words as someone who, like Samir, has done it himself—started, built, bought, and sold multiple businesses and someone who teaches entrepreneurship in an accredited business school. That's why I really appreciate the lessons Samir has captured in *The Millionaire Exit.* You won't get this stuff from any class.

You don't have to be a genius to succeed.

You don't need venture capital or an MBA from a prestigious business school. And you don't need a whole bunch of money or connections. You just need the right mindset, the right strategies, and the right guide. Samir is that guide. So read on! And here's to your success. Here's to developing your millionaire mindset—and millionaire exit!

—Mark C. Zweig, Author of *Confessions of an Entrepreneur*, Goody Award Winner for Best Book on Entrepreneurship, Chairman & Founder of Zweig Group, Entrepreneur In-Residence at Sam M. Walton College of Business, CFO/Director of Janus Motorcycles, Co-Founder of Mid-Century Modern Glassware, Co-Founder of Big Talk About Small Business, LLC, President of Mark Zweig, Inc., Director of Miyamoto International, Inc.

WHY THIS BOOK
IS RIGHT ON TIME

Congratulations!

You hold in your hands a book that's all about one thing: guiding you to not just start and grow a business but to exit as a millionaire. This isn't a dry business textbook. It's a toolkit, a real-world roadmap.

Inside, you'll find insights, steps, and strategies forged from my journey: from the days when I had nothing but grit and vision to the moment we sold our business for 200X our initial investment.

(In stock market terms, this is like selling the Amazon stock you bought in 2000—except we did it in 11, not 25 years.)

I am not a billionaire like Jeff Bezos (at least not yet), but I have enough money to not work for the rest of my life and not worry about my kid's future. I also have enough energy left over to make a positive impact on the world before my time is up. That can be your future if you follow the lessons I share in this book.

This book cuts through the noise. It's about the concrete steps, tough lessons, and quiet persistence it takes to build something worth millions and walk away with a whole lot extra in your pocket.

(Because, as I'm sure you've seen, there are plenty of PhDs who are barely paying their bills.)

Here's what you'll gain by reading this book:

1. You'll discover how to start a business right, steer it through the inevitable ups and downs to stay on a steep growth path, and make a successful transition when it's time to hand over the reins.
2. You'll learn how to handle finances, the art of scaling, and, most crucially, the powerful choices that prepare your business for a profitable exit.

Think of this book as the gear you need to scale a mountain most never attempt: a helmet, a rope, and a compass in hand. It's also your coach, whispering wisdom and hard-won lessons along the way.

You'll tackle quintessential questions that will shape your future, such as:

1. How do I build a great culture, make an impact, and be profitable?
2. Who will buy my business, and what's the best way to make it happen?
3. What will I do once my name is no longer on the door?
4. How do I build a legacy that's worth far more than just dollars and cents?

This book is your guide to growing and eventually exiting your professional services business as a millionaire. It's crafted for owners of small to mid-size firms, those under $10 million in revenue, who want to sidestep the common pitfalls and reach new heights, especially in today's ever-shifting market.

Imagine the peace of mind that comes from knowing you're prepared for every step of the journey—now and after your business is sold.

From humble beginnings to running a multi-million-dollar enterprise, my story is proof that you don't have to be extraordinary to create extraordinary success.

Ordinary actions, pursued daily with heart and consistency, build momentum. And this momentum transforms the seemingly small into the extraordinary.

Even though today, by all definitions, I am successful, I consider myself a late bloomer. I went through my trials and tribulations and climbed up the hard way.

Success isn't a finish line; it's a journey. And here's the good news: It's never too late to start walking that path. Whether you're in your twenties with a bold idea or your sixties with a lifetime of experience, success, and lasting happiness are always within reach if you're willing to pursue them with intention.

However, make no mistake: Success isn't handed to you. It demands courage to face uncertainty, wisdom to make tough choices, and the willingness to keep moving forward even when the road feels steep and unforgiving.

Yet the greatest secret of all is this: True success multiplies when you share it. When you teach others, mentor rising leaders, and give back, your success stops being just about you; it becomes a legacy. It grows, it expands, and it touches lives far beyond your own.

This book isn't just about building success. It's about building significance and doing so with a big dose of appreciation. Here's a taste of what you will discover:

1. How to develop a business that is sustainable and transferable
2. How to use your competitive edge to rise above the competition

3. How to empower your team so they can be efficient and innovative
4. How to build a sales and growth culture that doesn't depend on you
5. How to deliver consistent high-quality results that drive growth
6. Understand finance and benchmarking to grow company value
7. Know your options on this exit runway and choose wisely
8. Prepare your team and next-generation leaders for the transition
9. Choosing the right time to exit
10. Passing the torch and protecting your legacy

Any activity that makes the world a better place, especially one that benefits many people, takes money (unless you're Gandhi).

So, when you exit your business as a millionaire (or multi-millionaire), you will have the money to create a significant impact.

And if you're like me, creating success and impact is the lifeblood of being an entrepreneur.

√ Eighty percent of most small business owners' net worth is their business. Yet 70% don't know how to monetize. Avoid the pitfalls while moving toward profit (and purpose) at mybizmc.com/book.

DON'T BE A VICTIM
OF STATISTICS

Did you know that according to the US Bureau of Labor Statistics, as many as 20% of new businesses close in the first year, and more than 50% close within the first five years?

If your business is like most, you have a one-in-five chance of closing in the first year and a one-in-two chance of closing before year five.

If you have any hope of exiting, selling, or succession planning, you're immediately trying to climb a mountain in an endless snowstorm.

This book will give you the rope, the helmet, and a headlamp, not to mention a map, compass, and a GPS for orientation and planning.

Because if you want to exit your business as a millionaire, there are a few simple steps you can take to make sure your business starts and stays a success.

To leave a meaningful legacy and walk away wealthy, you must master these six essential questions every entrepreneur has faced:

1. How can you build a business that someone else will want to pay a premium to buy?

2. Do you sell the business to a few internal stakeholders, create an ESOP (employee stock ownership plan), or sell the business to an outside private equity firm?
3. How do you find a buyer with a culture that provides a future for your employees and allows you to be a subject matter expert (SME) and business leader without the stress of ownership?
4. What will you do once you are no longer the owner, decision maker, and visionary leader driving the growth engine?
5. How much is enough to ensure a secure retirement and generational wealth?
6. What kind of living legacy do you want right now? What kind of legacy do you want to leave behind?

While many options are available, you can be even more successful and impactful if you become a millionaire along the way.

THE NINE BIGGEST EXITING MYTHS

When it comes to building a successful business and eventually exiting as a millionaire, it is important to learn what to do as well as what not to do. There's no shortage of myths and misconceptions that can lead you off course. Let's clear up some of the most common ones, so you can focus on what really drives success.

Myth 1: If you build it, they will come.
A great idea is just the beginning. Success doesn't come from building alone; it's about connecting that vision with a real need in the market and executing with purpose. Similarly, just doing good work does not ensure business growth or success.

Myth 2: Working harder guarantees success.
While hard work is essential, it's not enough on its own. Success comes from working smart—making strategic moves, leveraging knowledge, and focusing on what matters most.

Myth 3: Risk-taking is the key to entrepreneurship.
Entrepreneurs may embrace risk, but smart entrepreneurs manage it. Calculated risks grounded in strategy drive growth.

This isn't about being reckless; it's about making informed decisions.

Myth 4: Business finance is complex and intimidating.
Finance doesn't have to be complicated. It's simple arithmetic at its core—revenue minus expenses equals profit. Knowing the basics and understanding the difference between cost and investment will empower you to make sound decisions that grow your business.

Myth 5: Hiring smart people is all you need for success.
Hiring talent is essential, but so is guidance. Your team needs your vision and oversight to channel their strengths in the right direction. Success doesn't happen on autopilot.

Myth 6: Financial success leads to happiness.
Money can bring comfort, but true fulfillment comes from meaningful connections, respect, and a sense of purpose. In business and life, it's not just about what we achieve but how we connect, lead, and contribute.

Myth 7: If you do good work, everyone will applaud.
Not everyone will see or acknowledge your hard work, and that's okay. Do good because it aligns with who you are, not because you expect applause. Staying true to your values builds inner fulfillment, and in the long run, that's what fuels sustainable success.

Myth 8: Cutting costs is the key to profitability.
Yes, managing expenses is crucial, but cutting costs without strategic investment limits growth. The goal isn't just survival; it's smart expansion. Identify where to cut and where to invest, so your business can grow stronger and more profitable.

Myth 9: Complexity equals growth.

Growth doesn't come from adding layers of complexity. Often, simplicity is more powerful. Streamlined processes, clear strategies, and focused goals allow you to scale effectively without getting bogged down.

Final thought: Success comes from clarity, simplicity, and staying true to what matters.

That means building and exiting a business as a millionaire isn't about following myths or trends. It's about making strategic decisions, simplifying where possible, and holding onto your values. In the end, success is about creating something meaningful, valuable, and enduring—on your terms.

HOW TO USE THIS BOOK

Congratulations on being here! You've already taken a significant step in your success, so let's keep going. This book is about growth, transformation, and the art of making things bigger and better.

- It's here to help you take what you've built and scale it beyond what you thought possible.
- It's about shaping a vision that isn't just yours but aligns with those around you, creating wins for everyone
- It's about resilience when life throws curveballs and maintaining the mindset that keeps you moving forward

This book will help you amplify what you already know so you can turn your expertise into something powerful and profitable. It's about developing the entrepreneurial spirit that will elevate you, whether you're building a business from scratch or driving innovation within an established company.

In all my years, I have never found a single resource that puts it all together. I had to gather insights bit by bit, from countless books, experiences, and lessons learned the hard way. That's why I've created this for you—to bring together the strategies, mindset, and practical steps that allow you to break through to the next level.

Read it start to finish or start with a key chapter. Just like how to start a business, there is no one right way. What fits you is the right way.

However, just like Mom used to say, you have to take at least two bites of each dish. So read each chapter twice. (They are easy to read and not very big.)

- Write down sections that resonate with you and put them up so you can see and remember them
- Tell others what you like and, more importantly, how you will translate that into an actionable plan
- Define a plan of action, but don't worry about the schedule if there is no external force to make you do it

Remember, all this wisdom didn't come from one sitting or from one book. It is a reiterative process of two steps forward, one step back.

Embrace that.

If you're ready to take charge of your life, to try something different and achieve more than you thought possible, this book is for you. Keep the right attitude and cultivate resilience, and you'll find yourself creating the success you've always dreamed of.

TAKING CHARGE OF YOUR DESTINY

A recent poll asked, "What's stopping aspiring entrepreneurs?"

An eye-popping 92% said lack of follow-through. They had the ideas—but they never acted.

Honestly, I wasn't shocked. I've known countless people just as smart (if not smarter) than me who talked a good game but never jumped. Even when they were miserable in their jobs, they stayed put.

Why?

Because the predictable present felt safer than the unknown future. Fear is a cozy prison, and they didn't have the guts to just do it.

If only they knew how ridiculously unprepared I was when I started—yet still ended up wildly successful.

On the other hand, many entrepreneurs make the opposite mistake: They're buried working in their business, not on it.

They trade freedom for a paycheck.

They end up with a lifestyle business—one that pays the bills but doesn't build wealth.

But the real prize?

An enterprise business: one with real, growing value you can sell or exit from as a millionaire.

If you want that outcome, here's the truth. It's not enough to read these pages. You have to act on them.

Stop waiting for someone to show up and tell you it's okay. You already have what you need:

- The courage to choose the uncertain path
- The willingness to build value, not just income
- The roadmap you're holding right now

Entrepreneurship doesn't reward those who wait for permission. It rewards those who figure it out, even when the path isn't clear.

If you want to cash out big, build your legacy, and change your life—take the next step.

No one's coming to save you. But you can save yourself. And this book will show you how.

THE PATH TO EXITING AS A MILLIONAIRE

D id you know that the bulk of the global economy is driven by small businesses, many of which are minority- and women-owned. Success (in starting, growing, and exiting) comes from thinking like an entrepreneur.

Did you know that 99.9% of all US businesses (33.3 million) qualify as small businesses according to the US Small Business Administration?

This number not only reflects the dominance of small businesses but also shows how they create jobs and contribute to economic stability, a trend that remains unchanged in 2025.

Whether it's owning a business or being a more innovative leader in an organization, this kind of entrepreneurial thinking is invaluable.

- It's critical for executives and leaders who choose to blaze their own path
- It's how you exit as a millionaire
- Especially if you're in the architecture, engineering, and construction industries

Heads up: The rate of failure for a small business is extremely high.

But it doesn't have to be.

That's another reason I'm writing this book.

And while you're about to receive a wealth of proven wisdom and guidance, I encourage you to connect with me for a conversation.

Because this is not a journey to be taken alone.

It will take time, but don't give up.

You can do this.

I proved it.

Throughout the process, I realized that a well-planned exit includes more than a financial windfall.

However, most M&A firms (mergers and acquisitions) don't have the bandwidth or interest in helping business owners build up pre-sale or walk with you post-sale.

They are interested in the deal and often lack the on-the-ground, connect-the-dots capability that will help you flourish and be attractive for acquisition and have a rewarding life after the exit.

MY MILLIONAIRE EXIT

My wife, Asawari, and I founded Code Unlimited in 2011. A well-rounded, one-stop shop for building code, fire code, accessibility, fire protection engineering, and performance modeling, Code Unlimited earned a reputation for reliable technical expertise with a focus on problem-solving and developing creative, customized solutions.

Within ten years, Code Unlimited grew into a multi-million-dollar business with more than 30 employees, spread across five offices in the Pacific Northwest and Las Vegas.

And somebody was paying attention!

Jensen Hughes, the world's largest building and fire code consulting services provider, acquired Code Unlimited in 2022.

We were able to sell the business and actualize the value that we had built.

Code Unlimited certainly did not become successful because of one person; it takes a village to raise a successful business. In this book, I have distilled the lessons learned and the strategies that succeeded against all odds, and there were quite a few challenges along the way.

One of the earliest decisions was whether a business partnership was detrimental to our marriage. We didn't know the answer going in, but looking back, we made some key decisions that ensured both the business and our marriage flourished. Those lessons apply to all partnerships, as business is truly like a marriage, and breakups are very painful.

A successful enterprise takes more than technical abilities; it requires leadership, vision, grit, management, and many other skills. Many entrepreneurs have a blend of all those abilities, but there are many examples of complementary teams of partners and key employees that have built successful businesses.

A successful exit is an even rarer accomplishment, as most entrepreneurs delegate that thought to the end of their journey, and by that time, it is often too late to get the great value they deserve.

This book will show you how to build a great enterprise and exit as a millionaire.

You won't build a business you can sell for millions without rolling up your sleeves and diving into the numbers: spreadsheets, financials, metrics. I've leaned on them to make data-driven decisions that moved the needle.

But here's the truth every seasoned entrepreneur learns: Sometimes you have to trust your gut. Intuition fills in the gaps that numbers can't explain.

Wisdom is knowing the difference.

This book is packed with both:

- The hard data you need to make smart, profitable choices
- The real-world insights that teach you when to follow instinct

Use these tools freely. Challenge yourself to master them. Ride them all the way to the kind of success that doesn't just pay you but pays off when you exit big.

If you want to sell your business for life-changing wealth, learn to balance the science and the art of decision-making. That's how you build something worth buying.

In the prelude to the book, I included what I consider "my universal truths" or "core beliefs." These are not business strategies but life lessons, which formed the foundation for my future business strategies. Except I didn't know them when I was building the superstructure.

They are easier to see now that I look back. When your wings get tested against the storms (and the storms will roll through), you will thank me for these insights.

What I call the immigrant entrepreneur mindset will help you build a meaningful business and set you on a path to success.

The immigrant entrepreneur mindset knows that there's no safety net, no fallback plan, and no one is coming to save you. It's the drive to succeed despite limited resources.

- It's the ability to navigate obstacles rather than crash into them
- When you hit a wall, you climb it or go around it
- When you face a river you can't swim across, you build a boat

This mindset isn't about brute-force resilience; it's about adaptability, efficiency, and strategy. It's knowing that persistence alone isn't enough; it's finding the path of least resistance to move forward.

I learned this lesson firsthand, starting from scratch more than once.

(I'll dig deep into all this in the following pages.)

When I started writing this book, we hadn't decided to sell Code Unlimited yet. Originally, the book was going to be all about how to start and grow a business.

Then the sale occurred, and I realized that most entrepreneurs know even less about exiting than starting and growing a business. The books I have read about both topics revealed a huge gap.

This book is my response to it.

I hope you enjoy it as much as I have enjoyed writing it.

I thought it would take me one year to write it. Almost three years later, it's ready.

Why am I sharing this?

Because this is how the life of an entrepreneur is. This is what I mean when I use the term resilience.

It doesn't mean I will work till I die, but I will not let go until I decide that it is not worth doing. There are plenty of ideas that I decided are not worth doing, so I am strategic about what I am resilient about.

The final and largest section is about exiting as a millionaire. These are the insights I gained and want to share about building a business that others value and are willing to pay top dollar for. I have seen too many owners burn out at the end and walk away from their most valuable asset because they don't know how to monetize it.

I don't want you to be part of the 70% of business owners who do that. If not, when you walk away wealthy, look me up, and we will have a nice glass of wine watching the sun set in a beautiful location somewhere on this planet.

THE 10 PRINCIPLES OF SUSTAINABLE BUSINESS GROWTH

E very successful business shares a secret; it doesn't grow by accident. It grows because its leaders follow a set of guiding principles that keep them focused, resilient, and ready to adapt.

This is what separates businesses that merely survive from those that truly thrive. From delivering premium value that commands top-dollar pricing to creating reliable processes that ensure consistency and excellence, these principles aren't quick fixes or trendy hacks; they're timeless truths.

Whether you're navigating growth challenges, preparing for a profitable exit, or simply trying to scale without breaking, this chapter will equip you with actionable insights to build a business that's not just successful today but sustainable for years to come.

Get ready to see your business (and your role as a leader) in a whole new light.

Here are the 10 Principles:

1. Premium Value – A successful business isn't built on scraping by; it's built on delivering premium value.

This means offering products and services that clients are willing to pay top dollar for, even in tight markets. Start with what your clients truly need and value, not just what excites you. Many businesses claim to be customer-focused, but few truly understand what their customers care about most. Real success lies in uncovering and delivering that value consistently.

2. Prolific Innovation – A thriving business doesn't rely on one product or service. Diversify your portfolio, even if it means variations on a theme. Keep innovating, improving, and staying ahead of the competition. Don't wait for others to close the gap; always stay one step ahead.

3. Purposeful Planning – Every goal, every project, and every milestone begins with a plan. Planning isn't optional; it's the foundation of sustainable success.

4. Relentless Practice – Like elite athletes, top-performing businesses refine their skills through consistent practice. Test your systems, sharpen your processes, and prepare for critical moments. Success isn't luck. It's preparation meeting opportunity.

5. Persistent Promotion – Don't rely on word of mouth alone. Constantly promote your business, your products, and your services. Your competition isn't resting, and neither should you. Your customers have choices, and external forces are always shifting. Stay visible. Stay relevant.

6. Resilient Perseverance – Success isn't a straight road; it's filled with setbacks and obstacles. Push forward with resilience, but stay adaptable. Perseverance isn't stubbornness; it's the ability to read the signs, adjust your course, and keep moving forward.

7. Strategic Pivoting – Knowing when to stay the course and when to pivot is one of the hardest decisions in

business. Sometimes you need an outside perspective—someone who can see your business without bias and provide clarity. Pivoting isn't failure; it's evolution.

8. Prudent Financial Management – Profit isn't just about revenue; it's about managing costs wisely and generating positive cash flow. Know the difference between cost and investment. Don't cut corners where it counts, but also don't spend recklessly. Smart financial decisions build sustainable growth.

9. People and Culture – Businesses don't grow without the right people. Build a culture that aligns with your vision and hire individuals who embody that culture. Don't hesitate to part ways with those who don't fit. Be cautious with equity; there are many ways to reward talent without diluting ownership too soon.

10. Reliable Processes – Processes create consistency, efficiency, and scalability. Build systems that produce high-quality results every time. Invest in the right tools, train your team thoroughly, and embrace project management. Strong processes protect your profit margins and enable growth.

When these 10 principles work together, they create sustainable, scalable, and profitable growth. This isn't just a business strategy; it's a blueprint for building something extraordinary.

√ Eighty percent of most small business owners' net worth is their business. Yet 70% don't know how to monetize. Avoid the pitfalls while moving toward profit (and purpose) at mybizmc.com/book.

NOBODY IS BORN AN ENTREPRENEUR

Was I born an entrepreneur?
Certainly not.
I went from young immigrant to successful entrepreneur, to senior executive at a global consulting company, to building generational wealth.

I've been on a journey that very few have experienced.

But wisdom is teachable, actionable, and will help you exit as a millionaire.

I see my life's journey in "The Road Not Taken" by Robert Frost. (Except I would change the word "sigh" to "joy" in the last stanza.)

I shall be telling this with joy
Somewhere ages and ages hence:
Two roads diverged in a wood, and I—
I took the one less traveled by,
And that has made all the difference.

Being an immigrant offered many powerful lessons.

During my studies, I worked the graveyard shift as a janitor in the student union building at the University of Oregon.

It was my willingness to do what it takes to succeed—even cleaning toilets.

It was this willingness to do the ordinary that was the centerpiece of how I achieved the success I did.

And it allowed me to finish college without any student loans and a savings of $1,500 (a large sum for a struggling student).

It was the collection of ordinary actions with determination, consistency, and persistence that turned into the extraordinary.

And they became the success principles I live by to this day.

No One Owes You: That's Your Superpower

Pop culture loves to tell the story of the lone genius—the entrepreneur who conquers all, fights the odds alone, and rides off into the sunset with a billion-dollar IPO. But let's be honest, that's not how most real businesses are built.

The immigrant entrepreneur mindset is different. And no, you don't need to be an immigrant to embrace it. It's about owning your reality, starting from exactly where you are, and seeing every inch of progress as something you earned.

It's the mindset that says, "No one's coming to save me. No one owes me anything. And yet, I will still build something extraordinary."

When your back is against the wall, you learn to value the small wins. You start seeing progress as fuel, not just proof. You measure growth in steps, not leaps. That's how you build staying power.

The Nine Pillars of the Immigrant Entrepreneur Mindset

Here's the truth most people miss: Million-dollar exits don't come from hype. They come from the daily disciplines, grounded systems, and gritty belief that success is built—not gifted.

Build from that place, and you won't just sell your business. You'll build something others *want* to buy and something that gets buyers interested *before* you even hang up a "For Sale" sign. Here are the nine pillars:

1. Make Magic with Limited Resources - Even when the tools are scarce, the vision stays strong. You learn to do more with less—and still come out on top.

2. Find the Canoe, Even if You Can't Swim - When others freeze at the edge of the river, you innovate. You will find a way across—canoe, raft, or sheer determination.

3. Choose the Path of Least Resistance (Not the Path of No Risk) - Instead of chasing a perfect safety net, you follow the current of momentum, practicality, and progress.

4. Don't Die on Every Hill - You don't need to fight every battle to win the war. You live to grow, lead, and sell another day.

5. Believe in Your Inner Resources - No matter what's thrown at you, you trust that your drive, skill, and resourcefulness will rise to meet it. And they do.

6. Reroute When the Wall Won't Budge - You don't bash your head against a brick wall forever. You go over it, around it, through it, if needed—and always forward.

7. Resilience Isn't Just About Endurance - It's about efficiency. Not every obstacle needs a battle. Sometimes the smartest move is the simplest one. That's how you scale and how you sell.

8. Turn Failure into Fuel - Every setback is raw energy, and you use it to power past the next hurdle.

9. Practice Appreciation - It's never too late to feel successful and happy in your own way.

MORE ON APPRECIATION

Appreciation isn't fluff; it's the foundation of everything I do.

Looking back, even in the lean early days, my wife and business partner, Asawari, was a constant source of strength.

We felt a deep sense of pride because we had enough.

We had a vision.

That belief in possibility lit our way forward.

That mindset didn't come from margin; it came from meaning.

And it was supported by the behind-the-scenes champions who helped remove obstacles and lighten the load.

Practicing appreciation reminds us that true wealth isn't just a number; it's the relationships that support, ground, and lift you.

It's the invisible infrastructure of trust and belief that no bank account can hold.

Don't overlook it because appreciation is a currency all its own.

Cultivate it, treasure it, and you'll find the journey and the success it brings are far beyond profit.

THE VALUE OF "FAILURE" IN GROWTH AND EXITING

Through my journey with starting, growing, and exiting, I learned that sometimes the best lessons come from what didn't go as planned—from the deals that lacked the right questions and the contracts that weren't quite solid. These experiences taught me not only what to do differently but also how larger firms navigate the complex world of mergers and acquisitions.

Lessons in Growth, Risk, and Real-World Success

At one of the firms I worked for early in my career, we went through a big accounting software change. There was fanfare, excitement, and high expectations. Then it fell flat. It was a complete failure. And honestly, I was surprised. This was a firm full of top-tier problem solvers and project managers.

However, here's what went wrong: No one treated the change like a real project. They handed it off to a team of IT and accounting folks who were technically solid—but they were not project managers. The outcome was missed expectations and a frustrated team.

That experience stuck with me. So, when we transitioned from QuickBooks to Ajera at Code Unlimited, we did it differently. We treated it like any other client-facing project—with a clear technical manager and a project manager. On smaller projects, it was one person supported by a senior leader. On larger projects, the roles were split. That structure created accountability, clarity, and strong communication. Our Ajera transition went off without a hitch.

Another early lesson was not to skimp on the tools or the talent.

At a previous company, I recommended investing in CFD (computational fluid dynamics) software and hiring an expert to gain a competitive edge. The leadership balked at the cost— and the opportunity passed. That company lacked vision.

When I started Code Unlimited, I took a smarter route. We sent two of our staff to learn from a university professor in Canada. We hired expert consultants to manage the risk. Our team gained confidence, and soon, we were winning the projects we used to lose—faster, better, and more profitably.

Big Firms Buy Alignment

Later, I learned a bigger strategic truth during the sale of Code Unlimited. Big firms don't just buy businesses; they buy alignment. They acquire skills, geographic presence, or niche expertise that fit into a long-term vision. They plan in five-year increments and make smart moves to fill gaps.

If you're looking to grow, think beyond organic growth. Consider strategic acquisitions. Yes, that means capital—but capital is out there, if you plan wisely. SBA loans can open doors, and private equity (PE) can bring not just funding but high-level guidance. Just know this: PE firms are only interested if your business is big enough to justify their time and money. Therefore, growth, again, becomes essential to valuation—and to your eventual exit.

Get help from someone who's done it. Find consultants who've walked your path and can guide you through it. With the right team, you can turn growth into opportunity and challenges into wins.

I've made mistakes. I've learned the hard way. And each lesson has sharpened my vision. If you treat failure like feedback and setbacks like steppingstones, you'll come out stronger and a whole lot closer to a millionaire exit.

FOR THE YOUNGER GENERATION: A DIFFERENT WAY TO THINK ABOUT EXITING AS A MILLIONAIRE

Today's younger generation is often laser-focused on building billion-dollar software empires. But here's the truth: Aiming for billions overlooks countless opportunities that can make you a millionaire—opportunities well within reach and built on tangible, solid businesses.

In our rush to chase the glamour of unicorn valuations, we forget there's a wealth of real-world success waiting in the millions, not billions. For many, becoming a millionaire is not only possible but also achievable with the right strategy and focus. And yet, the spotlight only shines on the mega-deals, leaving the steady, profitable paths to million-dollar exits in the shadows.

I give guest lectures in architectural colleges. I ask the students to raise their hands if they came to architecture school to make money.

Very few hands, if any, go up.

That's a problem; many architects end up being small business owners, and we are not preparing them for that journey. The same is true of other professions.

Architecture, engineering, medicine, and law are supposed to be noble professions where the practitioner is supposed to focus on societal good and not enrich themselves.

This preaching holds back many from achieving the financial success we so deserve.

This book is here to help change that thinking.

You can make money *and* make a difference.

The reality of business isn't always glamorous. It's often built on grit, steady growth, and making smart choices—not glittering billion-dollar valuations. And there's incredible freedom and security in reaching that millionaire milestone.

So, let's rethink success: Aim for what's achievable, impactful, and real.

SUCCESS DOESN'T HAVE TO LOOK EXTRAORDINARY

While finance and tech tend to dominate the headlines—complete with IPOs, venture capital, and billion-dollar valuations—there's a far less glamorous, but increasingly reliable, way to build significant wealth in America: owning and operating a traditional, regional business.

One such example is Olson, a small business owner in Minnesota whose flooring equipment company generates roughly $50 million in annual revenue. After a strategic acquisition of an Australian manufacturer, he and his family now enjoy the opportunities that come with sustained success—private school, international travel, and financial security. His income places him among the top 1% of earners in the US—those making at least $550,000 annually as of 2022, not including capital gains.

Economist Owen Zidar of Princeton University, along with Eric Zwick of the University of Chicago, coined a term for this group of high-earning business owners: the "stealthy wealthy." They're not launching the next unicorn or trading on Wall Street. They're running flooring companies, auto dealerships, dental practices, beverage distribution firms, and professional service businesses. And they're thriving.

Zidar and Zwick's research shows a growing trend: For top earners, the largest and fastest-growing source of income is private business ownership—not banking, not tech startups. From 2014 to 2022, the share of income generated by business ownership among the top 1% rose from 30.3% to 34.9%. At the very top—the 0.1%—that figure climbed to 43.1%.

To put that in perspective, those in the top 0.1% were earning $2.3 million or more annually in 2022. And nearly half of that income came not from salaries, stock portfolios, or hedge funds but from building and growing companies that serve everyday needs.

This data reinforces something many entrepreneurs have learned through experience: Success doesn't have to look extraordinary. Some of the most secure, impactful wealth is built by solving practical problems, delivering consistent value, and quietly owning a business that people rely on.

In a world full of noise, the quiet path—built on fundamentals, strategy, and service—can still lead to remarkable outcomes.

(Thanks to the *Wall Street Journal* for the inspiration for this section.)

TWO SIDES OF THE WORLD: MY ENTREPRENEURIAL JOURNEY

My entrepreneurial journey started in Mumbai while I was still a student of architecture. A friend's father, a civil engineer, wanted to build a vacation cottage in a rural area and asked if I'd design it. I charged him 5,000 rupees—just enough to cover materials and travel. The project didn't make me rich, but it was invaluable. I learned how to bridge knowledge gaps by seeking guidance, how to manage logistics, and how to think like a business owner.

To reach the project site, I took a train, a bus, and hiked for half an hour. Every step reinforced a lesson: Success isn't about having the perfect conditions; it's about making things work despite imperfect ones.

REINVENTING MYSELF IN THE US

Fast forward to my time as an architect in the US, I quickly realized that the profession wasn't a lucrative path. I didn't have financial backing or an established network to start my own practice. Worse, the industry was saturated—too many architects, too few opportunities.

However, I also knew one truth: The only way to earn what I was worth was to own my own business. The question was what kind of business. I analyzed my strengths, the market gaps, and what people would pay for. Eventually, I landed on a niche that few understood but everyone needed: building and fire code consulting.

To establish credibility, I immersed myself in the industry. I founded a Code Committee at the American Institute of Architects (AIA), gave presentations, and built relationships. Then, opportunity knocked. At the time, the US was consolidating three separate national building codes into one. I was one of the few experts who was knowledgeable in all three. The timing was perfect, and I took the leap to start my consulting firm.

THE BRUTAL REALITY OF BUSINESS

I expected my former employer to send work my way. Instead, they shut the door on me. Fortunately, my networking efforts paid off. My first big project was consulting for IBM in São Paulo, Brazil.

But running a business is about more than getting clients; it's about knowing how to manage, scale, and sustain it. I had no roadmap. Then fate stepped in. A client I was pitching pitched me instead, offering me a partnership in their firm. It was an incredible opportunity: I could learn the business side of consulting without risking everything. I stayed for six years, but eventually, I hit a ceiling. The company's culture and structure didn't align with my values, and the senior partners controlled the rewards. I knew it was time to move on.

Samir Mokashi, CEPA® M.Arch. Ar.

STARTING OVER, AGAIN

In 2012, my wife, Asawari, and I relaunched Code Unlimited—but this time, we did it on our terms. No outside partners. Just the two of us. We expected slow growth—maybe a few clients and, if all went well, hiring our first employee in a couple of years.

Instead, we hit the ground running. By the end of year one, we had generated $350,000 in revenue. Within six months, we had outgrown our basement and moved into a commercial office. We scaled quickly, winning multiple fastest-growing firm awards, including the Inc. 5000 in 2020.

Then, in 2022, we sold Code Unlimited to Jensen Hughes, a global consulting firm. I retired as their global service line leader for code and performance-based design in 2025.

Now, I am starting over again. This book is a companion to my new consulting business, Business Millionaire Club.

Entrepreneurship is a lonely journey; there is no one standing on the sidelines applauding as you build the business in the early years. This time around, though, I have the benefit of experience. I have walked this path before and know what it takes to get here. This is the second act of the play that is my life. I'm starting something that I am excited about and that lets me give back to fellow entrepreneurs.

Though this is a change of career at age 60, when most are thinking about retirement, there are many examples of those who launched successful businesses late in their lives. Harland Sanders started KFC at 62. Ray Kroc started McDonald's at 52. Chaleo Yoovidhya started Red Bull at 62. Jaswant Kular started Jaswant's Kitchen Indian Spice Blends at 60, and there are many more examples. Hopefully, I will add to this list and not be a footnote to it.

The process of writing this book has already connected me with clients. I fill a gap that other firms cannot; I combine practical wisdom with a willingness to meet you where you are on your journey.

Just like Robert Frost said in his poem "Stopping by Woods on a Snowy Evening," *But I have promises to keep and miles to go before I sleep.*

After you read this book, share your story with me; reach out if you would like to know more about my consulting services.

VALUE AND THE POWER OF GOODWILL

In business, people often tell you, "Be careful. Don't let others take advantage of you." And yes, that's important. However, in my journey, I chose to err on the side of being a good person. I chose to give those I trusted the benefit of the doubt. Looking back, that trust has been returned tenfold in ways that go beyond dollars.

My commitment was clear: Create an environment where people feel safe, happy, and able to succeed. That's my definition, and I held to it, even when it would have been easier to let go of those values.

Even when it meant taking some knocks, getting overlooked, or being undermined, I refused to change my standards just because others behaved differently. Those values shaped our business.

Consistency was another cornerstone. In a small business, maintaining quality across different skill sets is no easy feat. But as we grew, I focused on ensuring our values and standards remained embedded in every person we hired. We didn't aim to be just "very good;" we pushed to be the best. And that commitment set us apart.

Finally, we fostered a culture of creativity and innovation. We encouraged everyone to think differently and never settle for "just okay."

What if, instead of fearing failure, you ask, "How can I manage risk but learn from failure?" What if, instead of trying to be extraordinary, you simply committed to doing ordinary things extraordinarily well?

That's how we built something lasting—by staying true to our values, caring deeply about our customers, and never losing sight of the relationships that make it all worthwhile.

Developing the Immigrant Entrepreneur Mindset

Every business I started followed the same core principle: bet on your strengths, not your savings. I didn't have money to invest, and I refused to take on debt. My business had to be built on my technical expertise, industry knowledge, and sheer hard work.

This is the immigrant entrepreneur mindset. And you don't need to be an immigrant to embrace it. It's about:

- Starting lean—funding your business through skill, not loans
- Focusing on what others hate to do—finding work that people need to do but don't or can't do themselves
- Leveraging expertise to create demand—not just selling a service but becoming the go-to authority in your field
- Investing in people—hiring top talent and paying well, knowing that skilled employees generate high-value work
- Scaling smartly—not just trading time for money but creating a system where the business grows beyond you

Many small business owners fear hiring; they see salaries as an expense rather than an investment. But I realized that the key to growth was delegation. If I could train five analysts and charge just $20 more per hour than their cost, I could scale without burning out. And I learned that even when competitors left to start their own firms, they often failed—because being an expert doesn't make you a business owner.

Let's change that.

THE CORE OF HOW I DID IT

Most small business owners never break free from the job mentality. They remain trapped, working in the business instead of on it. I designed my business differently. My model wasn't the typical one-person consultancy or what is commonly referred to as a lifestyle business; I was building an enterprise business.

Instead of being just another consultant, I positioned myself as the solution to a major industry problem. Most architects hated dealing with building codes. I loved them. I knew I could turn that pain point into profit.

So, I approached clients with a simple value proposition:

- You hate codes, I love them
- Would you rather design beautiful buildings or deal with code officials?
- I'll make your code problems disappear—for a price

That clarity, combined with expertise, turned prospects into clients. And those clients fueled our rapid growth.

EXITING AS A MILLIONAIRE

Selling Code Unlimited wasn't just about financial gain; it was about creating a legacy. I built a company that could thrive without me, which is why it was valuable to a buyer. And that's what I want to help others do.

My next venture, the Business Millionaire Club, is designed to guide business owners toward successful, profitable exits. Because true wealth isn't just about how much money you make—it's about building something bigger than yourself.

Your business shouldn't just give you a paycheck.

It should give you freedom.

It should create wealth.

And when the time comes, it should be something someone else wants to buy.

That's the immigrant entrepreneur mindset.

That's the millionaire mindset, too.

And when you embrace it (and practice it), you can build, grow, and exit your business as a millionaire.

WHY CULTURE BEATS STRATEGY EVERY TIME

You've probably heard the quote, "Culture eats strategy for breakfast." Peter Drucker said it, and it's truer today than ever—especially for small businesses competing with giants for top talent.

Early in my career, and later while working at large consulting firms, I saw the same problem play out repeatedly. These companies weren't truly building consulting *firms*. They were just collections of individual experts, operating in silos. The busiest people—the ones billing at the highest rates—were swamped, often handling everything themselves, including clerical work. Meanwhile, junior staff sat idle, underused, and underdeveloped.

It was wildly inefficient and completely unsustainable.

When I had the chance to build my company, I did it differently. I built a culture—not just a business. I built a system where collaboration replaced chaos, where roles were defined by skill, not title, and where every team member could grow while contributing real value.

Here's what that looked like:

- We stretched senior talent across multiple projects, focusing their time where it mattered most.
- We paired junior staff with experts, giving them real responsibilities and on-the-job learning.
- We assigned tasks based on skill level, not hierarchy or job title.
- We fostered a culture of asking for help early and backing each other up.

Think of it as replacing the old assembly-line model with a dynamic platform approach. Everyone owned the outcome. If something went sideways, the team jumped in, solved it together, and learned from it.

This created a virtuous cycle:

- Senior staff focused on high-impact work
- Junior staff grew rapidly and gained confidence
- The team delivered more, faster, and at a lower cost
- Morale, trust, and loyalty soared

Everyone did more of what they loved. Everyone felt seen, challenged, and supported. And yes—profitability skyrocketed.

That's what happens when culture isn't just a poster on the wall but a system that empowers your people to succeed, together.

Show me a company with sustained year-over-year growth, and I'll show you a business built on a self-driven, collaborative culture.

At its core, entrepreneurship thrives on two things: the ability to take calculated risks and the discipline to execute with precision. But no one builds lasting success alone. The real magic happens when self-motivated individuals work together, combining their strengths to achieve something far greater than what any one person could accomplish alone.

SELF-DRIVEN AND COLLABORATIVE ARE NOT CONTRADICTIONS

Many assume that independence and teamwork are at odds, but the truth is, they fuel each other. A high-performing culture isn't about choosing one over the other; it's about building a system that allows both to thrive.

- Empowered Decision-Making - When leadership decentralizes control, employees make faster, smarter decisions based on real-time information. This agility keeps the company ahead of the competition.
- Shared Accountability - A strong team is one where each person can take bold action, knowing that others will step in to support and help them succeed.
- Leveraging Strengths - The best leaders build teams that complement each other's abilities rather than relying on lone-wolf success. This prevents burnout and maximizes efficiency.

The danger of an overly self-reliant culture is that it can create tunnel vision—individuals focused only on their tasks, missing the bigger picture. This creates turf mentality and jealousy, but a collaborative team multiplies potential, ensuring no one is operating in isolation.

BUILDING A TEAM THAT (OVER) DELIVERS—EVERY TIME

A company earns trust, credibility, and long-term clients when it consistently delivers on promises. And that's only possible when teams are structured to adapt, flex, and meet demand without unnecessary delays.

Here's what sets winning companies apart:

- A Culture of Confidence - Clients trust teams that deliver as promised, without excuses. This means building flexibility into your system so projects can scale up when demand spikes.
- Timely Performance - A rigid, uniform workflow puts customers at the mercy of your internal schedule. Many high-value firms value perfection over timeliness almost to the point of having a perfection snob culture. However, most clients value timeliness more than perfection. If they find another company that moves faster, you lose them.
- Risk Without Fear - To drive innovation, employees must feel safe taking calculated risks. This means fostering an environment where failure is a lesson, not a punishment.
- Accountability and Recognition - High performers need to be held to a standard of excellence, but they should also be rewarded—not just financially but through recognition, career growth, and a sense of purpose.

REWARDS THAT GO BEYOND MONEY

Financial incentives matter, no question. However, money alone doesn't build loyalty. A truly engaged team is one that feels valued beyond their paycheck.

Smart leaders structure rewards to include:

- Public and Peer Recognition - Whether it's awards, shout-outs, or industry-wide acknowledgment, appreciation fuels motivation.
- Work-Life Balance - People want careers that allow them to enjoy life, not just survive it. That means great healthcare benefits, more paid time off, retirement plans, and work flexibility.
- Professional Growth - The best teams stay engaged because they see a future. Investing in mentorship, skill development, and leadership training ensures people stick around.
- Community Impact - Employees take pride in companies that give back. Meaningful involvement in charitable causes fosters a sense of shared purpose.

What I've learned over the years is simple: People aren't just looking for bigger bonuses. They want to be mentored, supported, and championed. A great salary matters, but a workplace where growth and appreciation are part of the culture is where people stay and thrive.

THE ULTIMATE TEST: CAN YOUR BUSINESS RUN WITHOUT YOU?

Many founders work themselves into exhaustion, believing they need to be the driving force behind everything. However, if your business can't function without you, it's not scalable; it's a trap.

A culture of self-reliance and collaboration means:

- You can take time off without everything falling apart

- Clients remain happy because the team is equipped to handle challenges
- Your company continues growing, whether you're in the office or on vacation

Your employees are watching you. If you work yourself to exhaustion, some may try to follow in your footsteps—but many will walk away, realizing it's not sustainable.

The best companies don't just build businesses. They build teams that can carry the vision forward—with or without the founder. That's how you scale. That's how you exit on your terms. And that's how you leave a legacy that lasts.

We once hired a senior fire protection engineer who'd been chained to his business so long, he hadn't taken a vacation in years. He was used to carrying everything on his shoulders, convinced the whole place would burn down without him.

We introduced him to our culture: collaborative teams, shared responsibility, and the freedom to step away without fear of disaster. When he finally planned that first, long-overdue vacation, everyone told him, "Go. Don't worry. We've got this."

Naturally, just as he headed for the airport, a client called with an urgent problem. But this time, something different happened:

1. The call went to another senior team member, exactly as planned
2. That person brought in the colleague who knew the issue best
3. Together, they solved it immediately
4. The client was thrilled

Meanwhile, our vacationing engineer found out about the problem and panicked. He called the client, ready to cancel his trip. But the client said, "No need. Your team already handled it. Enjoy your vacation."

That's the culture we built: a business that runs without any one person holding it all up. That's true sustainability. That's freedom.

What Buyers Really Pay For

If you want to sell your business for top dollar—or just finally get your life back—this is what buyers really pay for:

- A team that owns the outcomes
- Systems that don't depend on you
- A brand that delivers even when you're gone

Imagine handing over the keys, knowing the engine will keep running—smooth, profitable, unstoppable. That's how you turn a job you own into a business someone else will pay millions to own instead.

The Myth of Total Freedom

I often see entrepreneurs online talking about how "entrepreneurship is the freedom to do whatever you want."

Let's be honest, that's a pretty fantasy. The reality is far less glamorous.

Sure, you don't have one boss anymore. Instead, you have many.

Your clients are your new bosses.

They set the expectations.

They make the demands.

And they're often tougher than any manager you ever had. They don't care about your other priorities, your family emergencies, or your need for sleep. They want results.

Entrepreneurship can feel like trading a single leash for a dozen.

The truth is, many who preach this "total freedom" narrative are either lying outright or lying to themselves. They've convinced themselves that working 24/7/365 without getting fired somehow equals freedom.

If that's their definition of freedom, more power to them.

However, if you want real freedom—the kind that lets you step away, sell your business for millions, or actually live your life—it takes something different:

- Systems that run without you
- A team that owns outcomes
- A brand that delivers even when you're not there

That's not a fantasy. That's the work. And that's what buyers pay top dollar for.

Don't buy the lie that entrepreneurship is endless freedom by default. Build the kind of business that *earns* it.

One of the most overlooked challenges of entrepreneurship is mastering the art of setting goals, creating deadlines, and following through with relentless discipline.

Think back to high school. Your days were mapped out for you. A curriculum, a classroom schedule, homework assignments—everything had structure. In undergrad, you gained a little more freedom, but the framework was still there.

By grad school, the scaffolding disappeared. You had to chart your course, set your deadlines, and find your rhythm.

Entrepreneurship is much the same—but with higher stakes.

People often say entrepreneurship offers freedom. You can control your time, your choices, and your destiny. While that's true, the flip side is this: You are responsible for everything. You must set the goals, create the deadlines, and hold yourself accountable. No one is coming to check your homework. No one is going to remind you of what's important.

Being busy is not the same as being effective. It's easy to fill your day with activity, but entrepreneurship requires you to focus on what truly matters—not just what's urgent. Prioritization is a skill, and like any skill, it must be practiced.

TOOLS FOR STAYING DISCIPLINED

Some entrepreneurs swear by calendars, others by to-do lists, sticky notes, or productivity apps. For me, it's about one integrated list—a single place where my work tasks and personal tasks live side by side. Why? Because life doesn't neatly separate into "work" and "home."

As entrepreneurs, we must remember that success in business cannot come at the cost of our relationships. Whether it's being a parent, a spouse, a sibling, or a friend, those roles are just as important as any business meeting or project deadline.

Years ago, I was a chain smoker. I tried quitting repeatedly, but I couldn't make it stick. Finally, I changed my approach. Before I quit, I told everyone who mattered to me.

That public commitment put real pressure on me. I couldn't stand the idea of letting them down.

It taught me something about myself: I naturally put other people's expectations above my own. Their requests always seemed more important, more urgent.

Instead of fighting that tendency, I decided to work with it. I used it strategically.

I began applying the same principle to my planning at work, especially to those critical but often neglected internal tasks—the ones that don't scream for attention because they're not billable, not tied to a specific client project, and not obviously profitable right now.

Instead of pushing them to "when I have time," I made them real priorities by treating them like commitments to others.

- I told my team what I planned to do
- I shared deadlines
- I invited accountability
- It forced me to deliver

That's the lesson. If your natural instinct is to prioritize what others need, use it to your advantage. Make your own important work feel just as urgent. Treat it like a promise you can't break.

It's one of the simplest, most effective ways to move the needle on the things that build a stronger, more valuable business.

CONTROLLING YOUR DESTINY

Here's a truth few people talk about: Entrepreneurship doesn't mean freedom from responsibility; it means embracing responsibility on an entirely different level. It is about controlling your destiny, not running away from responsibility. It can be hard to cultivate the discipline and the structure to achieve it, but getting it right leads to long-term success.

In a traditional job, you're accountable to your boss. As an entrepreneur, you're accountable to every client, every customer, every investor, and—most importantly—yourself.

Your clients are now your "bosses." Their needs, deadlines, and expectations become your responsibility. And sometimes, you'll meet those expectations even when the profit margins are thin because credibility, trust, and your reputation are your most valuable assets.

FREEDOM THROUGH RESPONSIBILITY

Don't become an entrepreneur because you want to escape responsibility. Become one because you want to own responsibility.

Entrepreneurship is about shouldering the weight of uncertainty, decision-making, and long hours. But here's the promise: If you carry that weight well, the rewards are unparalleled.

The financial rewards may not come immediately. The recognition might not arrive overnight. But when the time comes to exit—when you've built something of value, scaled it with intention, and positioned it strategically—the payoff is worth every ounce of sweat and every sleepless night.

Entrepreneurship isn't freedom from responsibility; it's freedom through responsibility. Own that truth, and you'll build something extraordinary.

DISAPPOINTMENT FUELS SUCCESS

Disappointments are a part of life, and in entrepreneurship, they show up regularly. I'm not just talking about the big, heart-wrenching failures—the deals that fall through, the clients that walk away, or the projects that crash and burn. No, I'm talking about the smaller, everyday disappointments: missed deadlines, overcommitments, forgotten tasks.

These little setbacks can pile up, building an emotional weight that drags you down if you're not careful. How you handle these disappointments defines your long-term success. To me, disappointment is the same as someone telling me, "You cannot do this." After the initial frown, it brings on a soft smile, my eyes light up, and then I get to work!

KNOW YOURSELF AND
HOW YOU COMMUNICATE

Let me share something personal. I work with a dietitian to help me manage my health and fitness. You might expect someone who's seen a fair share of success to be highly disciplined, laser-focused, and effortlessly consistent. But I'm not.

My rhythm is different. My energy comes in peaks and valleys. When I'm in peak mode, I'm unstoppable. I work intensely, achieve milestones, and make big moves. But then there are valleys—those quieter times when I slow down, recover, reflect, and recharge. And that's okay.

When I was younger, I would get irritated at "my slacker phase" as I saw it then. However, as I matured, I realized that is just how I work, and this phase lays the groundwork for my peak drive phase. I've learned to accept my valleys and to maximize my peaks. I focus on extending those periods of high performance while minimizing the length and depth of the lows. I don't fight my natural flow; I work with it.

But here's the key: I communicate. If I miss a deadline or fall short, I own it. I reach out to my team, my clients, or whoever's involved. I apologize sincerely, reset expectations, and recommit to the task. Clear, honest communication keeps trust intact and prevents small disappointments from snowballing into major failures.

You don't need to share every detail of how you work with your team or clients, but you do need to set clear expectations. They should know what they can rely on you for, how you operate during your highs and lows, and what success looks like when you're in your groove.

FORGIVENESS AND ACCEPTANCE

Entrepreneurs are driven people. We hold ourselves to sky-high standards, and when we fall short, the disappointment stings. But it's vital to learn to accept the ups and downs as part of the process.

You are not a machine. Machines operate at a fixed, predictable pace. Humans—especially entrepreneurs—are different. And that difference, that unique blend of creativity, drive, and resilience, is exactly why people come to you.

You are the special sauce in your business. Your personality, energy, and vision are irreplaceable.

USING DISTRACTED TIME FOR MILLION-DOLLAR IDEAS

I like to think of my approach to focus as a kind of window shopping for ideas. When you're window shopping, you're not hunting for anything specific, but if you spot something beautiful or useful, you stop. Maybe you buy it, or you make a mental note to return later.

That's how I've trained my brain to use so-called "distracted" time for productive work. When I find myself stuck, unfocused, or just grinding without progress, I don't fight it. I step away. I take a short walk or make a cup of coffee and let my mind wander.

During those breaks, my brain relaxes or, just as often, fires off unexpected flashes of insight. They aren't always polished or organized. Sometimes they're raw but valuable. I don't let them slip away. I jot them down—on paper, on a whiteboard, in an email to myself, in OneNote, or on my phone.

Later, when I'm back in focused, productive mode, I review them. Some ideas get tossed aside as useless wanderings. But many become the seeds of solutions, helping me organize or crack smaller parts of a bigger problem. Over time, I've found these scattered moments make tackling the big tasks far more efficient and less overwhelming.

By giving myself permission to step back and wander, I've built a rhythm that's sustainable and often surprisingly effective. It's a reminder that even our distracted time can be harnessed—if we know how to catch those fleeting sparks and turn them into real progress.

The goal isn't to eliminate the valleys entirely. That's impossible. The goal is to understand them, plan around them, and make them work for you.

Maximize your peaks. Use those bursts of energy and focus to push forward on big goals.

Accept your valleys. Use them to rest, reflect, and prepare for your next climb.

Own your mistakes. Communicate openly when you miss the mark and rebuild trust through action.

Stay human. Don't let the myth of constant productivity steal your joy or creativity.

Success isn't about perfection; it's about consistency over time. It's about showing up, being honest with yourself and others, and staying committed through the highs and lows.

If you can learn to manage your disappointments, you'll notice something remarkable: Your successes will grow—bigger, faster, and more frequently.

Embrace your rhythm. Own your unique process. And remember—it's not about avoiding the valleys; it's about mastering the climb.

That's the recipe for success. It's worked for me, and I know it can work for you, too.

Do You Even Need a Partner?

Bringing a partner into your business—whether at the start or during growth—can be a game-changer. Done right, a partner can share the risk, complement your skills, and drive the company forward. Done wrong, it can be a source of stress, conflict, and even business failure.

I've seen partnerships that flourished and those that imploded. My experience taught me one thing: Great partnerships start with alignment on values, vision, and communication.

When Asawari and I built Code Unlimited, we chose to stay a two-person ownership team because we shared the same values, had the same goals, and had the complementary skills needed for success. That decision was validated when we grew rapidly and achieved a high valuation at exit.

If we had brought in another partner, it would have been a high bar to meet our expectations. In the end, we never did, but we handsomely compensated a key employee who was with us from the beginning without making them a partner. This is a great way to cultivate partner-level loyalty without complicating the firm's administration—benefits without the shackles.

Why Most Partnerships Fail

Making someone a partner is a serious decision. It gives them not just rewards but responsibilities. If they are not ready, it can create more problems than solutions. However, there is nothing preventing you from sharing responsibilities and adding key stakeholders with skin in the game without giving away control.

Before you bring on a partner, consider this:

- Misalignment of goals - If you don't share the same long-term vision, your business will be pulled in different directions.
- Poor communication - If you don't share the same values, any discussion turns into an argument. Without the ability to have open, honest discussions, frustrations build, leading to conflict.
- Ego and control struggles - If one partner wants to dominate, others may disengage, creating resentment and inefficiency.
- Lack of clear roles and responsibilities - Unclear decision-making leads to confusion for employees and weakens leadership.

A toxic partnership is like a bad marriage - Employees feel caught in the middle, unsure of whom to follow. This confusion drains morale, slows progress, and damages the business. Avoid it at all costs.

Do You Need a Partner to Succeed?

At different points in your business journey, you may ask:

1. At startup - Do I need a partner to succeed?
2. During growth - Should I offer a key employee a partnership to keep them satisfied?

Partnership isn't the only way to reward key contributors. You can:

- Give a raise - Recognize and retain top talent without giving away equity
- Offer bonuses - Reward performance while keeping ownership intact

- Create stock options or phantom stocks- Provide upside potential without immediate ownership transfer
- Promote them into leadership roles - Give them authority without making them an owner

CORE COMPETENCIES AND PARTNERSHIP

Successful businesses typically rely on three or four key competencies, often referred to as the three-legged or four-legged stool:

1. Technical expertise - The ability to deliver exceptional products or services
2. Marketing expertise - The skill to attract and retain customers
3. Financial and business management - The knowledge to run operations efficiently
4. Project/people management (in some cases) - The leadership to manage logistics and teams effectively

When choosing a partner, look for someone who brings strengths you lack. If you already have all four competencies, you may not need a partner at all—but if you don't, bringing in the right person could be a strategic move.

However, beyond skill, a great partner must have:

- Emotional resilience - Business is tough. They need to weather challenges without crumbling.
- Financial resilience - If they aren't financially stable, they may make decisions out of desperation rather than strategy.
- A long-term commitment - A partner isn't a short-term hire; they should be invested in the company's long-term future.

THE POWER OF COLLABORATION

Some partnerships thrive because they create a multiplying effect—where the partners bring not only skills but also a deep emotional connection, allowing them to:

- Bounce ideas off each other
- Solve problems faster
- Divide responsibilities effectively
- Ensure no one person carries the full burden

This model is especially valuable for entrepreneurs with young families. A strong partnership allows for balance, preventing burnout and ensuring that business success doesn't come at the expense of personal life.

However, not all partnerships operate this way. Some follow a distributed model, where:

- Each partner runs their division independently
- Common resources (staff, systems) are shared
- Collaboration is limited to high-level strategy

This model is more common in older businesses. Modern businesses tend to embrace collaboration more deeply, perhaps due to generational shifts emphasizing teamwork.

Regardless of the model, successful partnerships require trust, transparency, and shared accountability.

I attended an M&A conference, and a founder of the engineering firm, John McAdam, did a presentation about how he gave stocks as an incentive, which resulted in gaining loyalty. John, the majority shareholder, kept 80% of the ownership and control of the firm.

However, his employees felt included and valued; they appreciated the gesture. That was a unique hybrid system. The challenge when you have a large group of partners is that it is incredibly challenging to build consensus.

HOW WE BUILT A STRONG BUSINESS PARTNERSHIP

When my wife, Asawari, and I became business partners, we knew we had a solid foundation of trust and communication—but running a company together brought new challenges. Here's what worked for us:

- Defining boundaries - We decided not to talk about business before 9:00 a.m., giving us time to just be a couple, a family unit, without being on the clock 24/7 as business partners.
- Clear roles and decision-making authority- Asawari managed finance and business operations. I handled technical and marketing strategy.
- Equal ownership (50/50 split) - Despite legal advice to structure it 51/49 to avoid deadlock, we chose equal partnership to ensure both voices carried equal weight.
- For major decisions, the responsible partner had the final say, but we always aimed for consensus.

This structure worked because it ensured:

1. Balanced power dynamics - No one felt overruled or undervalued
2. Efficient decision-making - Each of us had autonomy in our domain
3. Stronger collaboration - We built the business together, rather than one person dominating

Many partnerships fail because one partner takes over, leaving others feeling powerless. Our approach equalized the playing field, preventing resentment and ensuring long-term success.

What New Partners Must Understand

Bringing in a new partner—whether a minor or major stakeholder—requires setting clear expectations.

Many new partners make the mistake of:

1. Overstepping authority - Assuming ownership gives them the right to make unchecked decisions
2. Not grasping responsibilities - Not realizing that ownership is not a privilege, it is a commitment to grow the business and those around you
3. Ignoring company culture - Failing to integrate into the established leadership structure

Here's how to avoid these:

1. Educate incoming partners on the business model, financials, and expectations
2. Explain the importance of controlling emotions and the enormous consequences of misspoken words and actions as an owner vs. when they were a manager
3. Clearly define their role, responsibilities, and decision-making power
4. Emphasize that ownership is about stewardship—leading the company, not just profiting from it
5. Explain the financial consequences of mistakes on the entire organization, not just an individual, as it was when they were an employee

Great partnerships aren't just about financial success; they're about building a company where both owners and employees thrive.

FINAL THOUGHTS: SHOULD YOU HAVE A PARTNER?

Before bringing in a partner, ask yourself:

1. Do they bring skills the business truly needs?
2. Do they share my values, work ethic, and long-term vision?
3. Are they financially and emotionally resilient?
4. Do we have clearly defined roles, responsibilities, and decision-making processes?

A strong partnership can accelerate your success.

A bad one can destroy everything you've built.

If you decide to move forward, be intentional, strategic, and clear about expectations.

When done right, a partnership can create a business that's more profitable, more resilient, and, ultimately, more valuable at exit.

√ Eighty percent of most small business owners' net worth is their business. Yet 70% don't know how to monetize. Avoid the pitfalls while moving toward profit (and purpose) at mybizmc.com/book.

THE 10 KEYS FOR YOUR MILLIONAIRE EXIT

G rowth takes many forms, each with its promise and challenge.

There's organic growth, where you build from within and strengthen what you already have. There's growth through acquisition, bringing another firm under your umbrella to expand quickly. And there's growth by merging, joining forces to create something greater than the sum of its parts.

For owners with revenue under $5 million—or even under $1 million—this journey can feel like scaling a steep, unforgiving mountain. That's where I come in. I help small firms take their first steps toward true scale, guiding a business with $500,000 in EBITDA to grow or merge into a $1 million EBITDA firm. From there, we set the stage to keep growing and, ultimately, prepare for a profitable, life-changing exit.

In today's market, small business owners are fiercely independent. That spirit is admirable, but it often means lacking the resources, experience, or mindset to grow through collaboration. The truth is that this process is anything but simple. You don't just decide to sell and watch the cash roll in. It's a long, complex, hands-on journey.

However, the value of collaboration is unmatched. Finding the right partners can unlock doors to exponential growth and deliver advantages that make your business far more valuable when the time comes to sell.

As a consultant, I work closely with firms for two to three years, laying the groundwork, building sustainable growth, and positioning them for the kind of exit that changes lives. Along the way, these businesses make more money, and so do I. But the real reward isn't just the extra income; it's the freedom and opportunity that come with a well-earned exit.

Exiting your business isn't just about signing a deal; it's about creating a future where your hard work continues to thrive long after you've stepped away. Whether you're handing over the reins to a new owner, a leadership team, or a successor, one thing is certain: A successful exit doesn't happen by accident.

You'll learn more about structuring your finances, communicating with your team, and choosing the perfect timing to maximize your value. Most importantly, you'll discover how to leave not just with financial security but with the satisfaction of knowing your legacy is intact.

Here are the nuts and bolts (and we'll dig in further throughout the book):

1. The Evergreen Engine - Build Your Business to Outlive You Build a business model that is sustainable and transferable. A truly valuable business isn't reliant on your presence; it's built on people, processes, culture, and systems that endure long after you step away.
2. Own Your Competitive Edge or Get Left Behind - How to Stand Out, Win More Business, and Maximize Value Know what sets you apart. Why do customers choose you? Your competitive edge isn't just a feature; it's your secret sauce.
3. The Leadership Playbook - How to Empower a Self-Sustaining Team To scale a business, you must

change from a founder-led business to one where a team of leaders executes the founder's vision. A successful exit requires a team ready to lead without you.

4. Building a Book of Business So You Can Grow and Scale Without Limits - Word of mouth is not enough; you must promote your products and services and build a pipeline of new customers to build real value. It must be process-driven, not personality-based.

5. The Predictable Machine - Deliver High Value, Consistently Sustainable businesses aren't chaotic; they're methodical. Consistency is your competitive advantage.

6. The Financial Crystal Ball - Keep Impeccable Records Clear, transparent financial records aren't just paperwork; they're proof of your business's value.

7. Choosing Your Right Path Forward - ESOP? Private equity? Leadership buyout? Succession?

8. The Heartbeat of an Exit: Communicating With People and Managing Expectations - Take care of your people, and your exit will take care of itself.

9. The Timing Trigger - Exit at the Right Moment Timing isn't luck; strategy allows you to recognize when the conditions are primed for maximum value.

10. Passing the Torch and Protecting the Legacy - The Steward's Mindset. You're not just selling a business and assets; you're passing the torch and leaving behind memories.

When you integrate these 10 keys, you'll do more than sell your business; you'll create a legacy, secure your future, and leave on your terms.

You'll also ensure that your business doesn't just survive your exit but thrives because of it.

This book is here to help you map that journey. Let's talk about growth. Let's start building something bigger together. **And when you're ready to have a conversation, you can reach me at** www.businessmillionaireclub.com **or** BMC@ mybizmc.com.

KEY #1: THE EVERGREEN ENGINE: BUILD YOUR BUSINESS TO OUTLIVE YOU

Most entrepreneurs start a business to create freedom—financial freedom, time freedom, and the ability to control their destiny. But the biggest mistake they make is that they build a business that depends on them.

A business that relies on you for everything—decisions, client relationships, innovation—may survive, but it will never be truly valuable. If your business can't grow or function without you, what exactly are you selling when it's time to exit?

To build a high-value, sellable business, you must do two things:

1. Create a sustainable business model—one that drives growth at every stage
2. Create a transferable business model—one that ensures the company thrives even after you leave

SCALING BEYOND YOURSELF

Every business reaches critical growth milestones.

Going from a one-person operation to a five-person team changes everything.

Expanding to 10, 25, 50, 150, or 250+ employees requires shifts in leadership, processes, and strategy.

At each stage, the dynamics evolve; what worked before will no longer work at scale.

Many business owners don't anticipate these shifts. They think growth will be a straight line when it's a series of transformations. The key to navigating is understanding the fundamentals that make your business sustainable.

THE FOUR PILLARS OF A SUSTAINABLE BUSINESS

At its core, every scalable, transferable business is built on four essential questions:

1. Why did we start this company?

Your original mission is your North Star. Growth brings distractions—new opportunities, tempting side projects, and potential pivots. But if you lose sight of why you started, you risk diluting your brand, burning through resources, and weakening your market position.

2. What is our core product or service?

Successful businesses focus on what they do best. Adding services or products that don't align with your strengths can become a financial drain. Clarity on your core competency allows you to scale faster, maintain high margins, and keep your competitive edge.

3. Why do our clients choose us over the competition?

Seeing yourself through your client's eyes is your superpower. What problem do you solve better than anyone else? What makes your company irreplaceable? The stronger your differentiation, the more valuable your business becomes to clients and potential buyers.

4. Why do employees love working here?

In the early days, the company is the founder. Your personality shapes the culture. But as you grow, culture must be intentional. Companies with a strong, well-defined culture thrive; companies without one collapse under their own weight. And when it comes time to sell, a healthy culture significantly increases valuation.

PLANNING FOR THE EVENTUAL EXIT OF THE FOUNDERS

Every business should plan for the exit of its founders—even if it's just starting out. The challenge is predicting the future when you have no crystal ball.

Start with realistic but ambitious goals.

Bring in outside advisors who can challenge assumptions and provide industry insights.

Build a financial structure that supports reinvestment, ensuring sustainable growth instead of just chasing short-term revenue.

Too many businesses assume they will always operate the way they do today. But if you plan to sell at a premium, your business model must be adaptable. A transferable business doesn't just maintain operations; it evolves without you leading the charge.

THE TRAP OF "OUR WAY IS THE BEST WAY"

One of the biggest reasons business owners struggle post-sale is that they resist change.

From the day the company was formed to the day it is sold, the company culture has probably evolved significantly. However, when a company is merged or sold, the leaders often assume that if the new owners stick to their original blueprint, the business will succeed. However, large growth spurts demand changes in the ways of doing business to be successful at the next chapter of evolution. Companies that thrive post-acquisition:

- Understand that leadership, structure, and culture must shift
- Accept that different leaders will bring different goals
- Build a system that allows for change without losing core values

FUTURE PROOFING THROUGH STRONG INTERNAL SYSTEMS

A transferable business isn't just about products, services, or leadership; it's about systems.

A well-built business can withstand leadership turnover, economic shifts, and competitive pressure because it has:

- Internal training programs to develop and replenish top talent

- Institutional knowledge management so expertise isn't lost with employee turnover
- Resilient business operations that adjust to external and internal changes

One of the biggest mistakes small businesses make is failing to build these costs into their pricing. They compete on price, not value, eroding their margins and limiting their ability to invest in long-term growth. A company that only focuses on delivering a product or service without future-proofing itself will always struggle to command a high valuation.

GETTING TALENTED INDIVIDUALS TO THRIVE IN A TEAM-FIRST CULTURE

A business is only as strong as its people. However, talent isn't just about hiring smart people; it's about managing them effectively.

Highly talented individuals can be perceived as difficult. They think fast, move fast, and don't always have patience for slower decision-making. The secret to leading them is earning their respect.

Once they respect you, they listen. Once they listen, they innovate. Once they innovate, they drive your company forward.

However, great businesses don't just win with top-tier talent. They maximize the collective value of their entire team. Any company can succeed with an A-team. The best leaders make even their B and C players perform at a high level.

The goal is to create a culture where the entire organization moves in the same direction, no matter who is on the team.

Build a plug-and-play system where talent fits into well-defined roles.

Train employees in technical skills, soft skills, leadership, and collaboration.

Develop a culture of excellence, where performance is consistent, even with leadership changes.

Build a culture where asking for help is seen as ensuring the highest quality standard is met, not a sign of weakness—a culture that allows mistakes to happen but uses them as teaching moments.

Most importantly, the executive team must understand that technical expertise, project management, and team leadership require different skill sets. Experience helps, but if there is no underlying desire or skill, experience alone is not enough.

When you do this, your company doesn't just survive transitions; it thrives through them.

WHY BUILD A BUSINESS THAT RUNS WITHOUT YOU

Many business owners struggle after a merger or acquisition because they suddenly find themselves stripped of authority. They go from calling the shots to asking permission. The financial structure changes, and many founders quickly realize they make less money as an employee than they did as an owner.

This is why building a truly transferable business pays off.

To a savvy buyer, a company that can operate and grow without its founder is infinitely more valuable than one that needs them at the helm. The key indicators of a high-value, transferable business include:

- A leadership pipeline—so new managers step in seamlessly
- A knowledge-sharing system—so expertise doesn't disappear when key people leave

- A strong market position—so the company continues to attract new business
- Scalable processes—so operations don't break down as the business grows

This is how you build a business that survives—and thrives—without you.

YOUR LEGACY: A BUSINESS THAT OUTLASTS YOU

Even with the best preparation, post-merger integration must be actively managed. It requires:

- Founders stay engaged but not over-controlling
- A culture that embraces change rather than resists it
- A high level of internal communication to ensure alignment

The goal is a business that runs smoothly, grows profitably, and sells at a premium because it is not dependent on you.

That is how you build wealth, create freedom, and leave a legacy.

KEY #2: SCALING YOUR DIFFERENTIATOR

In today's crowded marketplace, being good isn't good enough.

You can be talented, experienced, and even brilliant—but if your prospects can't clearly see why you're different, you'll get passed over for someone who can tell a better story.

Most businesses blend into the background. They say the same things, promise the same results, and compete on the same playing field. But the companies that win are the ones that grow, scale, and sell for a premium. They stand out—on purpose.

Your competitive edge is not a tagline or a clever pitch. It's the real reason your clients choose you, trust you, and stick with you. It's what makes your business memorable, irreplaceable, and valuable.

In this chapter, we'll uncover what that edge looks like for you and how to turn it into your growth engine.

You'll discover how to move beyond vague marketing speak, like "We're innovative" or "We care about customer service," and define something that's real, specific, and hard to copy. We'll talk about how your edge might be responsiveness, industry certifications, deep local knowledge, or a service model so consistent it feels like magic to your clients.

You'll also learn why your edge needs to evolve as you grow and how to scale it in a way that increases your business value, boosts your pricing power, and positions you for a successful exit.

Finally, we'll explore how differentiation builds trust, drives referrals, and turns your expertise into recurring revenue—without needing to hard sell.

When you know your edge—and you know how to use it—everything changes.

Clients come to you.

Revenue grows without chasing.

Buyers line up when it's time to sell.

You don't just build a business. You build a brand people believe in and a company worth every penny of your asking price.

Let's sharpen your edge.

If you can't clearly define what makes your business different, your customers won't see it either.

Many companies default to generic answers:

- We're creative
- We're innovative
- We prioritize customer service

While these are nice statements, they don't set you apart. Your real competitive edge—the reason clients choose you over your competitors—is deeper. It's specific. It's the irreplaceable factor that keeps customers coming back.

If you don't know what that is, your business will stagnate. However, when you uncover and own your unique advantage, you create lasting growth, higher profits, and a company that commands a premium when it's time to sell.

FINDING YOUR TRUE DIFFERENTIATOR

Your competitive edge doesn't have to be extraordinary; it just has to be clear, consistent, and valuable to your clients. Here are some examples:

- Exclusive Certifications - If your industry requires a specialized certification that only a few firms have, that's a powerful advantage. Clients must come to you because no one else can legally or expertly provide the service.
- Peer-to-Peer Recognition - Many firms list their awards, but very few explain how they benefit their clients. That explanation of why the award mattered to the customer is relevant to future customers choosing your firm.
- Customer Testimonials - Many buyers are looking for affirmation from your customers as a means of separating two competing bids. Having them on your website and marketing materials helps.
- Responsiveness and Reliability - Some firms win not because they're the best but because they always show up. Clients trust them to answer the phone, solve problems, and meet deadlines. Reliability is rare and incredibly valuable.
- Deep Local Knowledge - If your business depends on established subconsultant relationships, local market expertise, and knowledge of difficult regulatory processes, emphasize that. Large competitors may have more resources, but they often lack on-the-ground connections and insights.
- A Systematic Approach to Service - For us, a key differentiator was consistency. Our clients knew that whether they spoke with a senior leader or a new team member, the quality of service never wavered. That didn't happen

by accident; it was the result of a structured training system and a company-wide commitment to excellence.

- Cost - This one always flies under the radar but is high on most customers' lists, even if they don't say it. They are not always looking for the cheapest, but the least cost best value. How to articulate that in your communications is the hard part. I have found that asking your customer, "Can you tell us how we provided value to you?" is a great way to get it in a way that speaks to your future customers.

Your differentiator is what clients notice, remember, and trust. The stronger it is, the harder it is for competitors to replicate.

Your Differentiator Will Evolve, so Keep It Fresh

What sets you apart today may not be enough tomorrow. Your edge needs to be continuously evaluated and refined.

If your advantage is price, someone will undercut you.

If it's a niche offering, competitors will catch up.

If it's expertise, your team must stay ahead.

That's why combining multiple differentiators makes it even harder to compete with you.

For example, when we launched our business, we were one of the few certified minority business enterprises (MBEs) in our field. That opened doors, especially for clients looking to diversify their vendors. However, once we got in, we proved our technical expertise, responsiveness, and deep industry knowledge—and that's what kept us as their preferred consultants.

As we grew, we strengthened our advantage by expanding regionally. Suddenly, we weren't just the best in one city; we were the go-to experts across the Pacific Northwest. National firms tried to compete with us, but they couldn't match our local relationships, insider knowledge, and rapid response times.

Your edge must grow with your business—or you'll get left behind.

DIFFERENTIATION IN ACTION: HOW WE USED IT TO SCALE FAST

Clients want predictability, not just expertise.

When we started hiring aggressively, we worried clients might feel uneasy about working with new team members. So, we asked our most loyal clients for honest feedback.

What they told us surprised us: "We don't always talk to the same person, but the service is always the same quality."

That was intentional. Every new hire shadowed senior staff, ensuring they delivered the same level of expertise. We also reassured clients by making it clear that our senior team was always accessible, even if they weren't on every call.

By delegating tasks to trained staff, we gave clients more value for their budget.

This reinforced trust and made scaling easier.

Speed wins business.

Most firms took too long to respond to new business inquiries. We saw an opportunity to stand out by being the fastest, most responsive team in the market.

Every time a request for proposal (RFP) came in, we acknowledged it within 24 hours with a quick call or email.

Within days, we either sent a proposal or set up a scoping meeting.

This responsiveness became a signature strength that clients couldn't get elsewhere.

We served small clients without losing profits.
For smaller firms with tight budgets, we took a different approach.

Instead of lowering our fees, we:

- Limited our scope—offering key advice while letting them handle the execution
- Gave them cost-saving options—like writing reports themselves while we reviewed them
- Positioned ourselves as their strategic partner—so when their budget grew, we were their first call

This deepened client relationships and led to more referrals and repeat business.

Million-dollar wisdom is not more information.
Clients don't always know the right people or processes, but we did.

When clients were stuck, we outlined exactly:

1. Who to contact
2. What paperwork to file
3. The fastest way to solve their issue

Often, this led to them saying, "Actually, can you just handle this for us?"

This turned expertise into revenue without a hard sell.

Many people confuse information with wisdom. It's a common mistake, but it's costly if you're trying to build a business that stands out and commands top dollar.

Clients don't want mountains of data or flashy jargon. They want expertise delivered in a way that's simple, clear, and immediately useful.

What they're truly buying is wisdom.

In today's world, information is cheap and everywhere. Knowledge is a step better; it's just filtered information. However, wisdom is something different. It's the art of giving people exactly the right information in a form they can understand and act on, so they get the most value with the least effort.

That's what your clients really want. And that's what will make them choose you over your competitors.

Your competition will often hide behind complexity. They'll pad their reports with unnecessary details, industry jargon, assumptions, and endless caveats that make their work hard to read and even harder to use. Don't fall into that trap.

Teach your team to do the opposite. Deliver clear, concise reports that cut through the noise. Share insights that matter, recommendations people can act on immediately, and solutions that save time, money, and frustration.

If you consistently provide true wisdom instead of empty information, you'll win your clients' trust and their business every single time.

SCALING YOUR DIFFERENTIATOR

If your competitive edge isn't scalable, your business isn't sellable.

Buyers and investors look for companies with:

- A strong market position - A reputation that commands premium pricing
- Repeatable processes - A business model that works without the founder
- Diverse revenue streams - A client base not dependent on a handful of customers

- A competitive moat - Differentiators that make the company hard to disrupt

A strong brand, reputation, and service model increase your company's multiples on exit, which means more money in your pocket.

THE POWER OF STANDING BEHIND YOUR PRODUCT

One of the simplest, yet most powerful, differentiators is backing your work 100%.

Companies like Nike and Apple don't just sell products. They sell trust. Customers know they're getting the best—and they're willing to pay a premium for it.

If you stand by your work, respond when something goes wrong, and prioritize long-term relationships over short-term profits, you create a brand that people believe in.

COST VS. VALUE: HOW TO WIN THE RIGHT CLIENTS

If a client is only focused on cost, they won't see your value.

If they understand value, they'll pay for quality.

If a prospect can't see the difference between you and a cheaper alternative, you have two choices:

1. Show them your value—not just in words, but in experience
2. Walk away

A strong business isn't built by chasing low-margin, price-sensitive clients. It's built by owning your worth and delivering unmatched value.

YOUR COMPETITIVE EDGE = YOUR GROWTH ENGINE

Define what makes you different.
Strengthen your advantage over time.
Scale your differentiator so your business grows beyond you.
When you do this, you don't just build a great business.
You build a business that lasts.
You build a business that buyers want to invest in.
You build a legacy and walk away wealthy.

√ Eighty percent of most small business owners' net worth is their business. Yet 70% don't know how to monetize. Avoid the pitfalls while moving toward profit (and purpose) at mybizmc.com/book.

KEY #3: THE LEADERSHIP PLAYBOOK: HOW TO EMPOWER A SELF-SUSTAINING TEAM

A successful exit requires a team ready to lead without you. Success after your exit depends on clarity. Build a strong culture, well-defined roles, and a confident team equipped to thrive with optimism and ownership. Equip them with clarity, confidence, and the tools to maintain your business's momentum.

Imagine stepping away from your business and watching it not just survive but thrive. That's the power of a self-sustaining team, one that carries your vision forward with confidence, clarity, and commitment.

No buyer wants to inherit a house of cards—a business where everything crumbles the moment you're no longer in the room. A successful exit depends on building a leadership team that's prepared, empowered, and equipped to navigate challenges without leaning on you for every decision.

In this chapter, we'll explore how to create a Leadership Playbook—a clear blueprint for roles, responsibilities, and culture. You'll learn how to transfer not just tasks but ownership of outcomes. Because when your team operates with purpose and clarity, your business doesn't just look valuable; it is valuable.

Think of a blueprint as the DNA of your business's future—a precise, replicable code that, when followed, allows your business to grow strong, healthy, and uniquely positioned to thrive long after you've stepped away.

Your exit isn't the end; it's the moment your team takes the baton and runs boldly into the future. Let's set them up for success.

A STRONG LEADER CAN LIMIT THE GROWTH OF YOUR TEAM

A common side effect of having a strong leader is that the team may wait for direction or affirmation from the leader for critical decisions. This can be a detriment to creating a self-sustaining business environment post-transition.

The key is to build confidence in your team and the next generation leaders before you exit. Building a culture where there is trust and understanding among the leaders and a belief that the foundation will not fail and that they have the tools to elevate the firm's success to the next level.

This is easy to say but hard to do. Most commonly, strong businesses have one or two strong leaders, and normally, it is the founders. The founders are indispensable in the early years and critical to the long-term success of the business, especially repeat customers. However, strong businesses thrive even after the founder exits.

Let go of the controls without losing control.

Once you hire a strong team and teach them how to be successful, you must let go of the controls. Focus on maintaining quality, not by micromanaging but by clearly communicating the vision and articulating the success criteria. You don't want to constrain the creativity of the team. Creating a strong culture that encourages and, more importantly, rewards creativity, taking calculated risks, and learning from mistakes is the key.

Allowing individuals to make mistakes by not punishing them for taking risks is important, but it's also important to instill a culture of learning from your mistakes. Prepare for success, but plan for mistakes to happen. Manage the degree of failure so it is not catastrophic when it happens.

Building a process-driven culture, not just a results-driven culture, is important. A combination of well-defined processes, collaborative teams, and high interpersonal communication skills enables consistent, successful outcomes.

BALANCING FLEXIBILITY AND STRUCTURE FOR SUSTAINABLE GROWTH

Creating structure and setting boundaries isn't bureaucracy; it's the foundation for a successful exit. Key people in your firm need clearly defined roles, and they must buy into the vision for what the business will look like after you're gone. Without clarity, work slips through the cracks. One person expects the other to handle it, while the other thinks the same. The result is that nothing gets done, or both jump in and clash, leading to finger-pointing, turf wars, and unhealthy competition.

Defined roles, a strong culture, process-driven execution, and a confident, well-aligned team are critical to building a company that runs smoothly once the founders step away.

A startup thrives on flexibility. People wear multiple hats, adapting to whatever needs to be done. A larger company needs a clearer structure and defined responsibilities. The trick is managing both without letting them collide. Flexibility and structure can coexist, but you need to be intentional about it.

When we started out, we had just two categories:

- Experts
- Helpers

That simplicity worked at first, but as we grew, we realized we needed more definition. We worried that too much rigidity would create a "not my job" attitude. Too much flexibility, on the other hand, risked burnout if people didn't have a way to say no.

Structure and boundaries also help with:

1. Training new people
2. Assigning tasks effectively
3. Delegating without confusion

As we scaled, we began writing formal job descriptions for the roles that needed filling. However, those couldn't be static documents. They had to show employees a path for career advancement, so they knew how to earn a promotion or a raise. It sounds simple, but it's anything but.

In well-established professions, like architecture and engineering, industry-wide standards make this easier. In other fields, it can be much harder. We struggled with it ourselves. Our simple billing structure with just four levels worked well for accounting but failed to give employees a clear growth path.

In the end, we chose a hybrid solution. We created loosely defined job classifications and descriptions but reinforced them with a strong culture and open communication to bridge the gaps. That approach helped us grow, train our people, and prepare the company to succeed even when we weren't there to manage every detail.

Although your firm may have different names and categories, here is a generic list of titles, roles, and explanations for why each is a distinct task. On small projects, one person may wear multiple hats for efficiency and cost savings. However, having a clear understanding of these as required skills necessary for success allows you to manage the process without needing to take over:

- Project Manager/Task Manager/Project Coordinator - This is a very key role. The person in this role has the entire road map of the task or project mapped out and makes sure that nothing breaks down in the execution.
- Leader/People Manager - This role involves managing the personalities involved and making sure that the process is equitable and enjoyable for all. In most firms, the project manager wears both these hats, but it is a different skill and, on large projects, may involve a separate person who is more skilled at it.
- Technical Experts/Supervisor - This is the person who knows how to get the job done and can probably do it all alone, but needs a team due to lack of availability, high bill rate, or both.
- Finance and Administrative Manager - Again, on most projects, this role is handled by a project manager, but it is a separate skillset that needs to be understood and acknowledged. This ensures the client is billed on time and makes sure the invoices are paid on time. This may be the same person or a different person who manages documents for the team. In the current digital world, everyone manages their own document filing, but that leads to duplicate filing or missing files because they are not on a shared server. This can result in higher server storage costs and wasted time in finding documents when they are needed without someone with the right skill being assigned this task and role.
- Marketing Expert/Client Relationship Manager - This is the most overlooked role in small- and midsize firms and even in large firms. This person makes sure the customer sees the value in the service that was provided. They also make sure the customer is heard and receives what they were looking for, not just what was in the proposal. They then get feedback from the customer

about how the project went to ensure they will return for an encore and add to the growing list of accolades and testimonials. Any complaints are properly addressed to ensure the customers come back.

- Technical Specialist - This is also where you accomplish the informal transfer of institutional knowledge and build the company's work culture. This is one of the most important roles and is often delegated to junior managers to manage. Top performing firms have their senior managers provide oversight, as this is where the rubber meets the road for the value proposition the firm promises to provide to its customers. This is often called "grunt work" in the industry, but most senior staff honed their skills doing this and learning how to do the job well in this role.

Another critical reality to remember is that not everyone on your team wants—or is cut out—to reach the top of their profession. Some people don't want the added responsibility or pressure of moving up the corporate ladder. That isn't a bad thing, as long as you recognize it and plan for it.

I've worked with many mid-level professionals who were incredibly effective and valuable right where they were. They trained junior staff, supported senior leaders, and kept the engine running. However, eventually, they hit their ceiling for compensation and career growth.

Some employees are content staying at that level. Others will need a clear explanation about why their salaries can't keep rising forever.

Some will understand and stay.

Some will decide to move on.

If you want to keep these high-value mid-level people, you need to design alternative compensation plans. These might be tied to performance, like rewards for coming in under budget, even if they aren't driving overall company growth. It's rarely one-size-fits-all; it's often a custom approach. The key is making sure they see and appreciate the company's effort to create a unique role that fits within the larger structure.

Meanwhile, founders must invest in teaching the next generation of leaders what to do and how to do it. This isn't about cloning yourself. If all they do is emulate you, you become the glass ceiling they can't break.

Your job is to encourage them to surpass you.

That means learning to shift your leadership style:

- Sometimes you lead directly
- Sometimes you step back and guide others
- Sometimes you do nothing at all, which can be the hardest part
- Sometimes you give them a detailed plan and encouragement
- Other times, you share the vision and trust them to execute their way

Your ultimate focus must be on empowering the next generation to create a self-sustaining process that doesn't depend on you.

For any buyer, the value of your business goes up when there's a clear succession plan and a real promise of success after you exit. Your firm will grow even more if you have someone ready to take your seat. If you don't, you're stuck with the daily chores that keep you from taking the business to its true potential.

A CULTURE OF UPWARD MOBILITY AND GROWTH

When we were growing Code Unlimited, people would ask me, "How do I get into your seat?" My answer was always the same: "You can have my seat today." The sooner someone is ready to take my role, the sooner I can move up to the next level.

Ambition to move up shouldn't feel like an existential threat. In a flat company, people get scared to lose their jobs. However, in a growing company, when someone rises, it opens a spot for the next person to step up. That's how you fuel real growth.

Taking on a role you're not quite ready for carries risk. You might fail. But when failure is treated as an acceptable, managed result, it becomes a learning opportunity. This builds a resilient team that can handle challenges that might overwhelm other firms.

You want a culture that accepts small failures but avoids catastrophic ones. Catastrophic failures are bad for business. However, if you create an environment where leaders can stumble, trip, and occasionally fall without disaster, you're teaching them to:

- Manage risk
- Ask for help
- Execute plans effectively
- Set and manage expectations

This approach also encourages collaboration and communication. Those skills are essential for overcoming adversity and achieving sustained growth.

In firms with predictable, repetitive tasks, roles can be well-defined and stable. But in growing companies, tasks are variable, and roles must stay flexible. That demands strong senior oversight to keep projects on budget and on time.

Leadership and management are different skills from being a technical expert. Some people are multi-talented and can handle anything. Others need to be matched carefully to the right task.

Sometimes the skill sets fit, but the personalities clash. In those cases, an experienced manager is essential for success.

If the skill is there but confidence is lacking, one-on-one mentoring can make all the difference. Some individuals are naturally confident. Others need support, feedback, and affirmation to fully deliver on their potential.

Mentorship and the Leader's Role

Mentorship is a two-way street. Early in my career, I actively sought mentors for specific skills I needed to learn. Later, as a leader, I looked for mentees to help them grow and strengthen the team.

When I worked at a large firm, I had five mentors, each one covering a different gap in my skills. At smaller firms where those mentors didn't exist internally, I reached outside for industry experts. I found the best results when I volunteered with industry associations or joined committees.

That approach gave me access to professionals who not only had the right skills but also shared my values. It also offered a safe, non-threatening way to connect with external experts without raising alarm within my company about fraternizing with competitors.

I took those lessons and built our internal mentorship program. I introduced my staff to external experts but chose mentors from client organizations or collaborating firms— avoiding direct competitors while still providing valuable learning opportunities.

It's the leader's responsibility to see what will truly make the team successful. Sometimes that means publicly recognizing someone's skills. Other times, it requires repeating that acknowledgment privately and publicly until it really sinks in.

Privately, you may need to help them navigate potential mistakes, manage unexpected challenges, and reassure them that if things go sideways, you'll be there to step in and fix it.

It's popular to say, "Hire the right people and get out of their way," but even the most talented individuals need:

- Guidance
- Regular reminders of their goals
- A clear sense of accountability

A leader's job is to:

1. Plan the project
2. Build a complementary team
3. Assign tasks to the right people
4. Execute effectively

If you, as the owner, want to take on a bigger role, step back, or eventually exit the business entirely, you need to build a team that can sustain itself without your constant direction.

That means ensuring your people can handle everything the company does without relying on you or other key leaders.

It all depends on:

- A clear, shared vision
- Strong, intentional culture
- Well-defined roles
- A confident team equipped with the right tools to drive success

That's how you create a business that grows, thrives, and becomes truly valuable to a buyer.

KEY #4: BUILDING A BOOK OF BUSINESS SO YOU CAN GROW AND SCALE WITHOUT LIMITS

Marshall Goldsmith wrote a book called *What Got You Here Won't Get You There*.

That's the nutshell of the entrepreneur's journey. What you need at the startup stage is not what you need when you are ready to scale or when you have a well-established, flourishing business.

At the startup stage, you are hustling to get your first client and then the next and the next. You don't yet know which aspect of your vision will resonate with whom among the large net you have cast for potential customers. At this stage, you have to broadcast as widely as you can that you are available to assist, and when someone shows interest, you try to sell your services or products to that person.

You establish your generic resume, your custom resume, and general company literature.

You put the word out that you are open for business.

You talk to a few potential clients but rely on word of mouth.

You go after open bid opportunities.

You do free giveaways to get a foot in the door.

When you start scaling, you've had a few years under your belt and have a general idea about who your typical clients are. In this phase, you want to make sure you keep your current clients and broaden the base. You still do not have a clear idea of how to be laser-focused on the audience you seek and how to entice them with what you have to offer:

- You go to a conference or two
- You win awards, get some public recognition for your work, and use that to leverage additional work
- You jazz up your website and start a marketing blog
- You place some paid advertisements in business journals
- You participate in some edumarketing events

But...

You still don't have a well-organized process for business development.

You still don't have data about what works and why.

You still are doing this on the side in between doing the "real work," so it picks up when the business is down and goes down when the business is good.

When you grow to the next level, make sure to get help from a professional business development team. This is a hard step for many professional service firms. Traditionally, these firms have operated as a collection of small firms under a big umbrella. The business development activity is directly tied to the ability of the senior staff, such as associate principals or principals, to bring in work, the doer-seller model.

Many of these firms are disproportionately tied to a few clients who give them the bulk of the work, which can be a high risk for the business. Anytime one of these clients leaves, it creates a big hole in the firm's revenues. That's why you see a lot of boom-bust cycles at these firms. This is not good for long-term value building, but that is another discussion.

However, if you can figure out what works best within your firm's culture and establish a professional business development culture, it will take a load off most of the principals who want to focus on doing the work vs. shmoozing with clients for potential projects.

Here is an outline that worked for us, and some that I have seen practiced in larger firms I have worked at.

- Have the data to come up with a strategy and make decisions
- Track your proposals submitted and won year over year
- Track revenue by clients and market type year over year
- Have a system
- Have functional CRM software or a client-tracking system
- Assign tasks and roles to individuals to ensure follow-through
- Have a system to track key performance indicators (KPIs) and/or objectives and key results (OKRs) at regular intervals, not less than once a quarter
- Establish financial rewards for achieving and exceeding targets
- Start forecasting revenue growth accurately—accurately is the key
- Break down the revenue forecast by clients, products, and markets
- Align revenue forecast with staff growth and/or technology upgrades
- Get outside help to bridge the knowledge gap associated with developing strategic plans that work

Like everything else, none of this happens overnight. You will have to find the right leaders, then develop a plan with a team, then convert that to a sustainable system, then ensure it gets executed as planned, and tweak it as you get more data and better insight.

It is not something you try and see if it works. This must be a perpetual activity until you get it to work well.

The only alternative to doing this is the very inefficient model of principals working 60 to 80 hours a week. On paper, the firm might look like a high-performing business, but this is not a good model for owners who want to exit as millionaires or multi-millionaires.

YOUR PERSONAL VS. CORPORATE BRAND

Most people don't realize that they can have a personal brand and a corporate brand and that these can coexist without conflict. It can be a force multiplier when used together.

Your value is more than just knowledge.

It's a blend of what you know, who you know, and who you are.

Your corporate brand is often tied to your title. That can carry weight, but its value fades if you change companies or retire. A personal brand, on the other hand, can last a lifetime. It lets your influence extend well beyond your current role or even your industry.

Building a personal brand isn't complicated, but it does require intention. You can develop it through:

- Online professional platforms
- Volunteering at industry organizations
- Sharing your expertise freely
- Helping others grow

Lending your technical knowledge and offering real help is one of the most effective ways to build a personal brand that's bigger than any corporate title.

I've done this throughout my career by volunteering in many ways, including:

1. Local professional association chapters
2. My alma mater
3. Community centers
4. Cultural organizations
5. Special technical groups
6. One-on-one mentoring for anyone who asked

These efforts didn't just strengthen my network; they built trust and credibility that followed me everywhere.

Investing in your personal brand is one of the smartest moves you can make. It's an asset that compounds over time, delivers opportunities you can't predict, and adds lasting value to everything you do—even long after you sell or exit your business.

BUILDING YOUR PERSONAL BRAND

The first place to build a brand is in the staff resume. Most firms do not pay attention to how an employee's capabilities and experiences are written up to create a unique identity or brand in a resume. The birth of a resume is when the marketing person comes to a new staff member and says, "Do you have a corporate resume?"

The common answer is, "No, I don't, and I don't have time to do this." Then they scramble to find projects that the person worked on over the last year and get them in the resume template so it looks pretty. This is the opportunity to write a short paragraph about why this person is a great addition to the team. Pay attention to details.

Similarly, the firm's webpages, blogs, and marketing materials are where the brand is getting its start. Again, I find that it is a very generic write-up, and not enough attention is paid to customizing or aligning with the project needs and the corporate brand. This is often because the firm does not hire the right experts and does not allocate the right resources.

If you start with bad copy, it is harder to overcome it. Pay attention to the small tasks if you want to look great and do it efficiently. Be deliberate and strategic if you want to be great. However, avoid being obsessive-compulsive about it, which is often what happens when the owner gets into all the details and bogs down the process.

LinkedIn has emerged as a dominant professional site that is quite versatile and user-friendly. It allows individuals to align their personal branding with the company brand. This is a good way to keep in touch with current clients and be visible to potential clients and industry colleagues.

Make sure that every new staff member has a LinkedIn page. It doesn't take too much to do. Then ask your staff to like your company's posts. These simple activities build your name recognition and overall value to the buyer. Have your marketing staff and BD principals get premium subscriptions, which have many benefits. They can use them to analyze potential clients and competition and track analytical data to understand what is working and what is not.

The current generation has blended professional and social activity so much that professional sites like LinkedIn have started looking like Facebook, Twitter or X, Instagram, etc. Though that is one of the ways to connect with your potential market, it is not so direct and fraught with disappointment, as it is not as reliable for generating B2B business for companies.

The traditional expert marketing or edumarketing through professional talks, podcasts, and experts' panels are good ways to build a brand, but not always great at predicting revenue stream or return on investment (ROI).

Annual conferences are a good way to get continuing education hours and expand your network, but again, they are not very great at predicting revenue stream or return on investment. We came up with metrics for a go-no-go decision and found it useful.

Targeted mass media marketing to customers looks attractive at first, but it does not provide a great return on investment either. If you don't have a direct relationship with a large customer, a media campaign does not get you in the door with them. Media campaigns are better directed at smaller clients, even though that is hard to predict and control.

I have heard so often that so and so is spending billions of dollars, if we go after them, we will get a piece of the pie. It has never worked. If you are in the industry and have credibility, then have a strategic plan to go after specific customers who have defined OKRs to decide when you pull the plug. This is where you need professionals doing this, not just some junior-level person.

It is important to recognize that having a big network does not mean you will get a lot of work. Many sellers don't know when to stop selling and how to close a deal. When putting a team together, make sure you have a closer on the team.

Common bread and butter for professional firms is the request for proposal or RFP process. I am still surprised by how many firms regurgitate what they did for the last few projects and do not customize their materials. Paying attention to the specific requests in the RFP and checking out what the customer has selected in the past can be a good indicator of what is needed to win the job.

For a company to be successful, both personal and corporate branding are valuable. To maximize the impact, you should ride the coattails of your clients and other firms that share your values. Return the favor by giving them a plug where you can.

STOP GAMBLING, START STRATEGIZING

When business slows down, most companies suddenly decide it's time to "do marketing." Sound familiar?

I remember one recession in a large engineering firm. A senior VP of marketing had a flash of brilliance: Everyone with downtime (which was just about everyone) would start making cold calls.

There was just one problem: There was no strategy, no training, and no alignment.

As you might expect, the results were dead on arrival.

Another time, in a midsize engineering firm that served the high-tech sector, a similar panic set in. The plan? Start creating marketing materials for a bunch of industries we'd never touched, reach out to companies we didn't know, and hope something sticks.

It didn't.

No traction. No results. Just wasted time and effort.

Why does this keep happening? Why do otherwise smart people try to brute-force marketing when the pressure is on?

Because they don't understand this simple truth: Effective marketing is never an emergency move.

Marketing that works is a long game, not a last-ditch effort. It requires vision for the future and strategy for the now.

You need:

- A clear direction and realistic goals
- Consistent, measurable action
- Data to drive decisions
- A trained, well-prepared team
- A strong internal foundation—before you need the revenue

When times are good, that's the exact moment to strengthen your marketing and diversify your outreach. However, most small firm owners let marketing slide until things get tight—and that's a costly mistake.

Even today, too much of corporate marketing is driven by charisma, guesswork, and a sprinkle of voodoo. That's not a strategy. That's a gamble.

If you want to grow—or sell—your business like a pro, start treating marketing as the team sport it really is. Train, plan, and play to win.

SALES IS A TEAM SPORT

Sales is often sold as a solo sport—the rainmaker, the hero, the one-person powerhouse. But the firms that grow fast, win big, and eventually sell well play as a team.

In the best-performing firms:

- Business development data is collected and shared across the board
- Training happens for everyone—not just the "stars"
- Campaigns are created together and distributed to all
- Boundaries are clear, so no one's stepping on anyone's toes
- Top performers get first dibs as a reward—not a monopoly

This isn't theory; it's structure, culture, and clarity in action Younger professionals often default to collaboration—more so than past generations. And thanks to tech, it's never been easier to share data and ideas across the company. But there's a catch: Most firms still reward individual results. And that kills collaboration—fast.

Do you want people to share leads, insights, and opportunities? Change the reward system. Build a culture where credit is shared among everyone who contributed to the win. Then support that culture with structure:

- Hold regular meetings to clarify who's doing what
- Avoid doubling up or confusing the client with crossed wires
- Use these meetings to let junior staff shadow senior team members—learning by doing
- Make space for handoffs: Let one team win the work, another team deliver it, and both share the win

Recognition should match contribution. Whether someone opened the door or closed the deal, if they helped move it forward, they deserve part of the credit. Set goals at all levels—personal, team, and company—so everyone's aligned and engaged.

When the company started growing, I had to delegate. It freed me up and gave others space to learn. But I quickly learned that not all delegation is strategic.

I was the face of the company. People bought because they trusted me. That brand equity mattered. I couldn't delegate that.

I also needed to stay close to the work—so I could speak fluently about what we were doing, why it mattered, and what we were capable of. Clients want stories, not just stats.

We spread the senior marketing expertise across more projects, and I focused on where I added the most value: relationships and storytelling.

The biggest lesson was to keep it simple. Build real relationships. Pay attention to the details. Listen to the customer.

And always keep an eye on the market; it's changing whether you like it or not.

LEADING WITH STRENGTH

The old school model is making every person an all-rounder. If they have a weakness, then you work hard at eliminating that. This is great when it works, but there are several problems with this approach, especially in today's work environment. It is too slow, as it takes time to train an individual, which isn't there in today's ultrafast world. This can also create all generalists and very few specialists to push the excellence bar higher.

The leading with strength model brings together a team where each member is a specialist at their role and willing to work together with other experts. All the experts often have decent proficiency at a few other skills, so they can be back-ups or fill slots where expertise is not needed or an expert is unavailable.

You can have junior staff who are not yet proficient or other non-technical staff who are generalists do tasks that don't need experts. This allows the experts to focus on what they do best and spread across multiple projects without needing to spend a lot of time on each one.

This applies in all aspects of the business. In the business development context, somebody might be good at writing, somebody might be good at the visual aspects, somebody might be good at number crunching, somebody might be good at talking and presenting, and somebody might be good at maintaining relationships. All these skill sets are essential to building a business and getting and keeping clients.

We had a critical meeting where we needed a technical expert who was also good at storytelling. None of our principals was available due to scheduling conflicts. This was when we were still very small. We picked two staff members; one was a technical expert and the other a good communicator.

We coached them, explained their roles, and sent them to the meeting together. The client was very impressed. The technical expert spoke for five minutes, the communicator spoke for 20 minutes, the client spoke for about five minutes, and the meeting was half an hour long.

This approach also takes into consideration what interests those working on the project. If someone is interested in working on something that they are not an expert at but makes them happy, treating them as a generalist for this purpose and also tasking them with a job that is their expertise area makes it a win-win situation.

However, to make sure that all the parts are assembled correctly, there has to be communal ownership of the entire project. That way, no one is pointing fingers at each other. No matter who has the particular job, it is the job of everyone to deliver the complete project on time and meet or exceed the quality expectations of the company.

I've met many new clients when a current client comes up to me at a gala event and introduces me, "This is Samir Mokashi from Code Unlimited. I highly recommend them for all your code work."

That is always amazing to experience, but it is important to remember in these circumstances that it was the collective work of everyone doing their part that built the relationship and was the basis for the accolade. The technical team, the project managers, the admin and accounting support, the business development manager, and the marketing leader all play their parts and come together to weave a magical pattern.

Don't assume that all new business comes from the sales and business development team. That's why we call it a team sport and emphasize that internally and externally.

INCENTIVIZING FOR GROWTH: INDIVIDUAL VS COLLECTIVE

Business development is commonly a salary-based and commission-based compensation structure. How you establish the goals and measure success can be very important to the success of the individual and the team. Ideally, you want to make it an individual win measure in areas where you are currently not strong. However, where you have an established presence and there are other contributors, you want to focus on the collective measure. You can do this by market, region, or client. Also consider short-term versus long-term strategy.

I have always been a proponent of individual goals and collective reward sharing based on collaboration among team members and understanding the contribution of the silent members. However, when it comes to financial rewards, it gets hard to share.

At Code Unlimited, we allocated certain minimum points toward individual achievements, some toward benefiting the collective, and the rest were flexible and discretionary. This ensured that there is an established value to sharing work and crediting others, yet we could celebrate the individual's achievements and contribution to collective success.

You cannot get away from the KPIs (key performance indicators) or OKRs (objectives and key results) as the basis. During our employee reviews, we graded individuals for individual performance, their contribution to the group, and their contribution to the company. This way, we kept the focus on getting to the end collectively, that working together is better than working alone.

We also came up with the strategy to give credit to both vs. splitting up the credit as most firms do. So instead of 50/50, it was 100/100; the numerical calculation is the same, but the social and emotional rewards are several times better.

It is common for firms to assign billing targets or utilization targets to their technical staff, but for senior staff, revenue is also a secondary or sometimes primary target. For business development, it is almost always revenue targets.

The challenge on large projects is determining whether the client relationship won the project or the technical expertise won the project. It is best if both get to win; that way, both continue to work together and keep winning again and again.

Healthy competition can be good, but when it gets excessively competitive, it can undermine the company's social framework. A common example is a person working in one region of a market sector has an opportunity to introduce their colleague from another region or market sector, but does not even think about it, or, worse, does not want to do it for fear of competition.

Then, when the market is down and the company or the individual needs help, the relationship or the culture does not exist. When there is a toxic work culture, the star employee often leaves and will not tell you the real reason for their departure. That's the reason we didn't incentivize offices by their local revenue but by total company revenue, and then we gave them kudos or points for collaborating with somebody else.

If the incentive was improving the bottom line of the company across the board, then everyone would be willing to help someone else when their workload is light or their market is down. A good system has an incentive structure that prioritizes the individual's effort but sees it in the context of the subgroup, then the department, and then the company, in that order.

KEY #5: THE PREDICTABLE MACHINE: HIGH VALUE, CONSISTENTLY DELIVERED

Every successful business—no matter the industry, model, or market—shares one quiet, unshakable trait: consistency.

Not flashy. Not dramatic. Not headline-grabbing.

Just reliable, repeatable, and remarkably powerful.

Consistency is what transforms a scrappy startup into a sellable enterprise. It's what gives clients peace of mind, employees direction, and you—the owner—something rare in the entrepreneurial world: breathing room.

Too many entrepreneurs build a business that looks great on the outside but only functions because they're constantly holding it together. They're the problem-solver, the closer, the fixer, the glue. But what happens when they step away? The cracks show, things fall apart, and the value disappears.

This chapter is about building something that doesn't fall apart—something that lasts.

Because when your business runs predictably, it becomes valuable.

You'll learn how to create systems that deliver excellence repeatedly without needing you to micromanage every detail.

We'll explore how to build processes that are simple enough to be repeatable, yet strong enough to support growth and innovation.

We'll talk about how consistency at the component level, not just the big picture, creates space for customization and creativity—without sacrificing efficiency or quality. You'll see how even the most innovative businesses rely on deeply consistent systems to deliver what they promise every single time.

Most importantly, you'll discover why consistency is the foundation of a business that can run—and grow—without you. That's what buyers are looking for. That's what allows you to sell for a premium.

Because when consistency becomes your standard, everything else gets easier.

Profits rise. Stress drops. People trust you.

And you, the founder, are finally free to grow—or gracefully exit—on your terms.

THE LAUNCHPAD FOR INNOVATION

Back in high school, I was torn between two career paths: engineering or architecture. I chose architecture because it gave me more room to be creative. So, it might sound strange when I say that consistency is the launchpad for innovation. But it's true.

At the University of Oregon, and later in my professional life, I kept running into the same lesson: Quality is the foundation for real creativity and lasting innovation. Without that foundation, innovation just becomes noise. It's flashy, maybe, but forgettable.

A one-of-a-kind painting can stand alone. But applied art—like architecture or technical consulting—needs to be reliable, repeatable, and respected. That's what earns trust. That's what earns business.

In a small company like ours, we didn't have deep pockets for wild experiments or blue-sky research. We couldn't afford to innovate just for the sake of novelty. So, we got smart about it. Here's what worked:

- We treated every project as a chance to get better
- We used each new engagement to refine and evolve
- Innovation happened step by step, not all at once
- The best ideas came from the work, not outside of it

Eventually, those small improvements added up to major changes. But they were grounded in what worked. And more importantly, they were sustainable.

If we had reinvented the wheel every time, we'd be inconsistent, expensive, and out of business. Innovation without discipline leads to burnout, confusion, and broken systems. In contrast, consistency gives you a strong base to build from—project after project, client after client.

When you commit to excellence as a habit, innovation stops being a gamble and starts becoming a strategy.

If you want to build a business that lasts—and one that someone else will want to buy—you need one thing above all: consistency.

Consistency is what transforms chaos into clarity. It's what builds loyalty, strengthens your reputation, and allows you to grow without losing control. Without it, no matter how talented your team is or how brilliant your service may be, your business will struggle to scale, and even more so to sell.

Whether you sell products or services, the ability to deliver quality, innovation, and efficiency—reliably—is what separates thriving businesses from those just getting by.

Consistency doesn't mean everything has to be robotic. You can still customize. You can still innovate. In fact, the most innovative companies are the most consistent because they build repeatable systems at the component level. They standardize the foundation so they can get creative at the edges.

Here's what that looks like in action:

1. You develop repeatable processes
2. You improve individual steps without disrupting the whole
3. You build systems that are efficient and scalable, yet adaptable
4. You create a structure where technology enhances speed, accuracy, and quality
5. You train your team so no one person is irreplaceable
6. You give yourself the freedom to focus on growth instead of putting out fires

And here's the best part: You don't need expensive software or fancy consultants to get there. You can start with pen and paper, whiteboards, spreadsheets—and most importantly, your team's insights. Simplicity leads to clarity. Clarity leads to action.

However, for all this to work, your culture must support it. Predictability is only possible when ego takes a backseat to improvement, when ideas can come from anywhere, and when simple isn't dismissed as boring but respected as the foundation for brilliance.

Consistency is not the enemy of innovation.

It's the launchpad for it.

Because when your business runs like a well-oiled machine—day in and day out—you can finally step back, breathe, and build something bigger than yourself. Consistency is essential for delivering quality, innovation, and efficiency, all of which are very important to any business, whether selling products or services.

Top-notch businesses value consistency and repeatability. They also understand the importance of having a culture that will accept and encourage it. They promote a culture where ego does not get in the way of a good idea. Those who don't have such a culture won't have innovation, collaboration, and continuous learning.

To build the right culture that supports a predictable culture, some may call it a boring culture, takes great wisdom and open communication.

Explaining why simple and consistent are not boring but foundational for innovation and creative problem solving takes wisdom.

To deliver consistent quality over a long period, you must develop processes that are repeatable and predictable.

Consistency and repeatability do not mean you cannot innovate or customize

You can have custom solutions while standardizing the process.

You can improve an individual component or a set of components within a system without jeopardizing the entire operation.

Once you have a predictable system in place, you can innovate by:

1. Manipulating the logistics of the delivery
2. Managing the number of hours, required skill level, or number of steps required
3. Inserting technology to improve quality or shorten production time or both
4. Doing it in-house vs. outsourcing it, developing a training program to replace those who leave, and adding teams to expand capabilities, etc.

The number of innovations you can introduce once you have consistency and predictability is enormous.

HIGHER PROFITS, HIGHER EFFICIENCY, AND LOWER COSTS

Once you have a predictable system, you can manage the cost and price at which you can sell to your customers.

Once you have a predictable system, you can delegate the management to someone else so you can focus on growing the business.

You can grow the bottom-line revenue by selling more or increase profitability by improving margins on the same product or service.

This is why having predictable systems is an essential component, not just for cost-competitive businesses but also for high-value, high-profit businesses. Any business will benefit from having systems that are predictable.

To achieve this level of predictability, you must learn to simplify your processes and systems.

The key is to engage those who are familiar with the processes on a regular basis in the analytical exercises. You need a culture of continuous improvement so any changes can be implemented rapidly and effectively.

Consistency delivers high profits. Consistency delivers growth. Consistency delivers assurances. Consistency delivers predictability. Consistency reduces stress. Consistency removes uncertainty about the future. This is the foundation of a successful company.

KEY #6: THE FINANCIAL CRYSTAL BALL: KEEP IMPECCABLE RECORDS

Most entrepreneurs start with passion, hustle, and a vision. They focus on getting clients, doing great work, and growing fast. But too often, they overlook the one thing that determines long-term success and the ultimate value of their business: the numbers.

Financials aren't just something you hand off to your accountant or revisit during tax season. They're your dashboard, your roadmap, your early warning system, and your crystal ball. If you want to sell your business for a life-changing amount, you must learn to read, track, and master your numbers before you need them.

In this chapter, we'll reframe financial clarity as your greatest advantage, not just at the exit but at every step of the journey. You'll discover how simple, smart financial systems can help you:

- Track profitability in real-time
- Track and manage cash flow regularly
- Eliminate waste and increase margins
- Delegate with confidence

- Plan for growth with precision
- Most importantly, sell with power

We'll look at the most important metrics that buyers care about and how to make sure your financials don't just tell a good story but tell the right one. From multi-year trends to cash flow, pricing models to debt collection, this chapter shows you how to turn your financial data into strategic insight.

You'll also see why clean books and simple systems don't just help you run a smoother business; they make your business more attractive and valuable to buyers. A company with clear, predictable financials earns trust. Trust earns higher offers.

This isn't about complexity. At its core, business finance is about addition, subtraction, and disciplined decisions. You don't need a CFO or a degree in accounting to get it right. You just need to care, track the right numbers, and take action.

Do that, and you won't just run a business; you'll build a sale-ready asset that gives you freedom, wealth, and peace of mind.

Let's open the books and look into your future.

TRACK EARLY, TRACK WELL, TRACK SIMPLY

Like many of us, I didn't get much of a financial education in school. High school? Nothing.

College? Still nothing.

So, I had to learn it on my own.

Years ago, when Asawari and I started our family, we enrolled in a personal finance class at a local community college. The teacher had us track every expense—every single one. Suddenly, all the "little things" we used to overlook started adding up. That moment left a lasting impression on both of us. It's one of the big reasons we became so disciplined about tracking our business finances from day one.

As a lifelong reader of business books, one lesson kept hitting home: If you're making decisions without data, you're flying blind—and you're going to crash.

In my early architectural firm days, I was constantly frustrated by how disconnected the document labeling systems were from the actual business of serving clients. These systems were often designed by IT folks, accountants, or librarians. They made perfect sense on paper—organized by dates, serial numbers, or document types—but they were completely useless when trying to find work related to a specific client.

If we're running a client-focused business, why was our entire documentation system focused on anything but the client?

That question became the foundation for the project naming convention we created.

It wasn't just about tracking data. It was about aligning everything with our core mission: serving the client. That's what set us apart.

We built a system that:

- Made tracking simple and intuitive
- Connected every file back to the client
- Kept our team focused on what mattered most
- Turned organization into a strategic advantage

That's the real secret. Tracking isn't just for the accountants. It's a leadership tool, customer service tool, and profitability tool.

When you track early, track well, and track simply, you give your business the foundation to grow, serve, and scale.

Most entrepreneurs start their businesses focused on getting clients, delivering great work, and growing revenue. Few spend time thinking about financial tracking, cost management, collections, or forecasting. Then, as the business scales, they realize—too late—that without financial clarity, they're flying blind.

The most successful businesses don't wait until they're big to get their financial house in order. They start with a simple, structured system from day one.

Here's what worked for us:

- A unified system - We tied together our invoice numbering, project codes, and internal file structure so everything was organized by client name and industry sector.
- Consistency across departments - Our accounting, project management, technical, and business development teams all spoke the same financial language.
- Rapid access to client history - When a client called, we could pull up past projects, payment history, and interactions instantly, making us look sharp, prepared, and invaluable.

This may sound basic, but most small businesses don't do this. Many systems are designed by accountants who prioritize dates and project sequences over client relationships. Yet, when a client works with you, they see one company. They assume you know everything about them. When your financial and project tracking is structured around them, you create a seamless, high-value experience.

BEYOND REVENUE: THE REAL MARKERS OF SUCCESS

Many small business owners obsess over revenue growth—but revenue alone isn't the best measure of success.

Profit margins matter more.

A business growing at breakneck speed with razor-thin margins is under constant stress. However, a business with strong margins can be just as profitable—without the chaos.

Another common mistake is confusing costs with investments.

Hiring is often seen as an expense, so founders delay it, working long hours instead of smart hours.

The real question isn't how many hours you work; it's where you spend them.

Founders who delegate early gain the freedom to work on the business, not just in it.

Smart hiring fuels growth, boosts profitability, and creates a business that doesn't collapse from burnout.

CUT THE FLUFF, KEEP THE POWER

I've always believed in cutting through the noise. Simplicity isn't just a style; it's a strategy. Whether it's technical, creative, or financial, I've found that clarity leads to action, and action leads to results. I have a natural ability to spot patterns where others see chaos, and I use that skill to streamline systems so they actually work. That same mindset drives how I write: clear, concise, and practical. Especially when dealing with complex technical reports, I can't stand bloated binders full of fluff. If you can say it in 50 pages, why bury it in 400?

This same approach shaped how I built the financial and administrative side of the business. Simplicity wasn't just a preference; it was a performance tool. By removing complexity and keeping systems lean, we created clarity, speed, and consistency in the way we operated. That's what gave us control over our numbers, confidence in our decisions, and room to grow. Simplicity is more than aesthetic; it's what makes strong financials possible.

At Code Unlimited, we started with QuickBooks and a great CPA who set up our books correctly. As we scaled, we moved to Ajera, which integrated proposal development, project management, and invoicing.

We also grew our accounting team—not to create bureaucracy but to free our technical staff from admin work so they could focus on what they did best: delivering high-quality work and serving clients.

The result was that every invoice was accurate. Nothing was misplaced. No revenue was lost.

Our philosophy was simplicity wins.

A business's operations will inevitably become complex as it grows. Your financial systems shouldn't.

Too often, business owners leave financial organization to an accountant who focuses only on accuracy and compliance—not efficiency. That's a mistake. Financials should be simple, actionable, and strategic.

WHY WE TREATED ACCOUNTING AS A PROFIT CENTER

Business finance isn't rocket science. At its foundation, it's simple:

Money in.

Money out.

It's addition and subtraction.

If you track those numbers well, you can layer on deeper analysis—benchmarks, multipliers, competitive comparisons—but without simplicity at the core, complexity will strangle you.

ACCOUNTING IS REVENUE-GENERATING

Most businesses see accounting and financial tracking as overhead.

We saw it as a revenue-generating function.

Instead of burying financial tracking in administrative costs, we built it into our project budgets and billed for it.

Some of the benefits included:

- Lower overhead costs
- Higher profitability
- A financially sustainable support team

By doing this, we created a lean, efficient company that was attractive to buyers.

WHY SIMPLICITY SELLS BETTER THAN COMPLEXITY

As I've said before, the power of simplicity and clarity in business can't be overstated, especially in a world that grows more complex by the day. This belief wasn't just a personal preference; it shaped everything I built. It showed up in the way I managed my company, the way I communicated with clients and regulators, and ultimately, in how we demonstrated value to potential buyers.

Simplicity and clarity weren't just nice to have; they were strategic assets. They created confidence, transparency, and trust. And when it came time to exit, that approach made all the difference. It allowed buyers to see exactly what they were getting and why it was worth top dollar. Clear systems, clean books, and a well-run business are what turn a company into a valuable asset someone else wants to own.

When we went to sell our business, our financial discipline paid off.

We had:

1. Crystal-clear records—showing how diversified and stable our revenue streams were
2. A detailed financial package—demonstrating our efficiency and profitability
3. A strong EBITDA multiplier—maximizing our sale price

Many entrepreneurs only know what they deliver, but don't fully understand how they deliver it.

The most valuable businesses master both.

Here's what winning businesses do:

- Value sales and marketing in good times and bad times
- Invest in technical excellence—not just when things are slow
- Train people before the market shifts—not after
- Understand where the money comes from, where it goes, and what actions drive profitability

MASTERING MONEY AND METRICS

Managing money isn't about complexity; it's about precision and discipline.

1. Keep records accurate
2. Build financial systems that are simple and scalable
3. Focus on profitability over revenue

Do this, and you won't just run a business. You'll own an asset worth selling.

Many entrepreneurs love the thrill of building their business—serving clients, developing products, and innovating in their industry. However, when it comes to tracking financials and key performance metrics, too many business owners treat it as a chore—something to be delegated or dealt with later.

That mindset can cost you millions when it's time to sell.

If you want to maximize the value of your company, you must track and understand your business data over multiple years—not just when you're ready to exit. Buyers don't just look at a single profit and loss (P&L) statement; they examine multi-year trends to assess growth, resilience, and profitability.

It's time to overcome the mental block around financials and embrace the numbers as your roadmap to a high-value sale.

THE METRICS THAT MATTER: WHAT BUYERS LOOK FOR

Whether you're planning an exit in two years or ten, tracking the right data will increase the attractiveness of your business and improve your bottom line today.

(Make sure to have at least three years of records available.) Here's what to focus on:

1. Financial Metrics - The foundation of business value
2. Profit Margins - A strong, consistent margin signals efficiency and profitability
3. Revenue Per Employee - A key indicator of productivity and operational efficiency
4. Invoice Payment Cycle - How long it takes clients to pay—shorter cycles mean better cash flow
5. Bill Rate Multiplier - Measures how well your company prices and delivers value

Pro Tip: Buyers typically request three years of financial data. If you don't have solid records, start tracking now to build a clear, compelling picture of your company's performance.

INDUSTRY BENCHMARKS: KNOW WHERE YOU STAND

If you don't know how your numbers compare to industry standards, you're operating in the dark. Great firms track more metrics than those listed above. More data means better insights.

Seek out industry reports. I found Deltek's AE industry report invaluable; it helped us benchmark our company against competitors. It is available for free, but it is a year older as the data collection happens a year prior.

Establish your metrics. If industry data isn't available, build your own benchmarks based on historical trends within your company.

Tracking industry trends over time helps you identify strengths, weaknesses, and opportunities for improvement—all of which impact your valuation.

CLIENTS WANT TO BE VALUED, NOT JUST SERVED

As a business owner, I have hired plenty of consultants over the years. I never chased the cheapest option; I was always focused on value. You get what you pay for, yes—but I also learned that the most expensive doesn't always mean the best. That principle shaped how I made decisions, and I noticed that our clients approached things the same way. They weren't hiring us based on awards, flashy branding, or industry buzz. They were looking for something more personal, more grounded. They wanted to know that we valued their business as much as they did.

That realization changed everything. It was my aha moment—the turning point where I saw clearly what separated average firms from the great ones. Clients weren't impressed by prestige; they were impressed by genuine care and operational excellence. That became our edge. We couldn't outspend the big firms on marketing, but we could outperform them where it mattered most: execution, results, and client focus. Our job was simple—be exceptional at what truly mattered to our clients. That's how we competed. That's how we won.

Beyond financials, buyers look for operational excellence because a well-run company is worth more.

Here's what they're watching:

- Client Response Time - How quickly do you respond to inquiries?
- Proposal Turnaround Time - The speed at which you submit bids impacts win rates.
- Employee Efficiency - Are your teams structured to maximize productivity and revenue?

Key Insight: Employee efficiency is not utilization. It is the ability to get to the right answer in the shortest time. This influences the client satisfaction index. Many clients won't tell you when they're dissatisfied; they'll just leave. Tracking client engagement metrics helps you improve retention and command premium pricing.

Smart Pricing: The Key to Long-Term Profitability

One of the biggest profit killers is underbilling.

Most technical staff underestimate the time spent on projects. They don't account for small, essential activities—meetings, emails, or even a coffee break. This, in addition to not valuing their personal worth and the hourly rate at which they bill, results in underbilling.

Fixed-fee projects help stabilize revenue and ensure you're paid for the full value of your work.

The Solution: Instead of relying on employees to track hours accurately, create efficient task management systems and build fair pricing models that align with real project costs.

CASH FLOW AND DEBT COLLECTION: PROTECTING YOUR HARD-EARNED REVENUE

You've done the work, now make sure you get paid.

Follow up on invoices immediately. Don't let late payments slide.

Charge interest on overdue invoices. Clients who delay payments increase your risk; hold them accountable.

Consider debt collectors as a last resort.

Be willing to walk away from bad clients. If they consistently pay late, they're costing you more than they're worth.

Even though your contract allows you to sue someone for lack of payment or not meeting the legal agreement, consider that option carefully. It is notoriously expensive and time-consuming.

Your employees and good clients shouldn't suffer because a few bad clients delay payments. Protect your cash flow, and your business will stay strong.

YOUR CLIENTS' WORDS WILL SELL YOUR BUSINESS

Once a serious buyer finishes looking under the hood, they'll turn to something less tangible but just as critical—how your customers feel about your business. They'll want to hear, directly from your clients, how well you deliver, how much value you bring, and whether they'd work with you again.

This is the kind of credibility that can boost your valuation with a higher multiplier. And no, it doesn't happen overnight. However, if you have two or three years before your planned exit, there's still time to shape this narrative. Start by putting strategies in place that consistently improve the client experience. Shift your customer satisfaction from average to excellent. Reach out directly to key clients, clean up any past issues, and reset the relationship. A strong reputation isn't just nice to have; it's an asset that pays off when it matters most.

Metrics matter—but so does perception. Buyers want to see credibility, authority, and a strong reputation.

Powerful examples include:

- Awards and Recognition - If your industry doesn't have awards, create credibility through rankings (e.g., "Fastest-Growing Firm") or high-profile projects.
- Community and Board Involvement - Encourage employees to serve on industry boards or local organizations; it elevates your firm's status.

Reputation takes years to build—but can tarnish in an instant. Operate with integrity and never make claims you can't stand behind. Your values get multiplied by the actions of your staff; always be ethical in your interactions.

BUSINESS VALUATION, COMPENSATION, AND RETENTION

Talent retention is a major factor in business valuation.

- Salary vs. Bonus Structure - Competitive salaries prevent poaching, but bonus structures align employees with company growth.

- Defined vs. Discretionary Bonuses - Be transparent—employees often expect bonuses, even if they're "performance-based."
- Collaborative vs. Individual Incentives - Misaligned incentives can create internal competition instead of teamwork.

Bottom Line - A well-structured compensation plan keeps top talent engaged, making your company more attractive to buyers.

AN OVERLOOKED COMPETITIVE ADVANTAGE

Many businesses cut training costs to save money, but that's a mistake.

Invest in training as a core business strategy. A skilled workforce produces higher-quality work and better client outcomes.

On-the-job training equals billable work. Just like apprenticeships in construction, training should be integrated into project budgets, not seen as overhead.

A well-trained team improves efficiency, reduces errors, and increases long-term profitability.

SHARPEN THE AXE

There's an old saying attributed to Abraham Lincoln, the 16th president of the United States:

"Give me six hours to chop down a tree, and I'll spend the first four sharpening the axe."

Your business metrics, pricing models, financial tracking, and operational efficiency are the blade that determines how effectively you cut through the competition—and how much your business is worth when you sell.

This means:

1. Track the right numbers
2. Improve your internal processes
3. Position your company as a top-tier acquisition

If you do this, you (happily) won't have to time the market; you'll be ready whenever the right buyer comes along.

√ Eighty percent of most small business owners' net worth is their business. Yet 70% don't know how to monetize. Avoid the pitfalls while moving toward profit (and purpose) at mybizmc.com/book.

KEY #7: HOW TO GET MAXIMUM VALUE FOR YOUR BUSINESS

Every great journey needs a map. And when it comes to exiting your business, the path you choose isn't just a road; it's your legacy. Should you hand the keys to trusted leaders through a management buyout? Create an ESOP to empower your employees? Or perhaps attract private equity for a high-stakes growth play? Each route has its peaks, valleys, and milestones.

However, there's no one-size-fits-all exit plan. The right path depends on your vision, your values, and the future you want to create—not just for yourself but for your team, your clients, and the business you've built with care.

In this chapter, we'll unpack each exit option, weighing the pros, cons, and potential outcomes. You'll gain clarity on which path aligns with your goals and learn how to navigate the decisions that will define your legacy.

The map is in your hands. Let's chart your course—step by step.

FOUR MAIN EXIT PATHS

When it comes to selling your business, there are four primary routes:

1. Selling to Private Equity (PE) - Typically, a mix of cash, stock, or assets
2. Selling to Internal Leaders - A buyout by key employees or partners
3. Transitioning to Employee Ownership (ESOP) - Employees purchase shares, often financed through a bank loan
4. Keeping It in the Family - Passing the business to the next generation

I considered all four. My son had once been interested in fire protection engineering, but later pursued a different path, eliminating the family business option.

Internal buyouts, whether through leadership or ESOP, were problematic because my team didn't have the capital for a full purchase. That would mean financing the sale through a PE firm, bank loan, or deferred payout plan (taking from future profits) with significant risk if the company struggled post-sale.

So, we pursued a private equity sale.

What I Wish I Knew Before the Sale

We ultimately sold our company to Jensen Hughes, a global leader in our industry. The timing was excellent. We attracted multiple interested buyers, but Jensen Hughes made an above-market offer before others could compete.

Our M&A broker, however, didn't push for competing bids—a decision I now see as a missed opportunity.

Lesson: Always explore multiple offers. Competition drives higher valuations.

This realization is why I'm launching Business Millionaire Club—to fill the gap in advisory services for small-mid market businesses with under $2 million EBITDA and under $10 million in annual revenue.

The market for under $1 million EBITDA and under $5 million revenue is the most challenging, as these businesses are unprepared for an acquisition. Above that, they are somewhat prepared but get undervalued without the right guidance.

Most M&A firms focus on closing deals fast in the small-mid market. They don't provide the white-glove service that high-net-worth clients receive. And because most owners only sell once, brokers aren't incentivized to prioritize long-term relationships.

That's the reason I picked this market, and as you can imagine, I have a soft corner for these entrepreneurs. I have been mentoring a few of them and seeing the difference it makes.

Great customer service is the foundation for strong client relationships—even in one-time transactions. I am betting on that as I start this new venture.

WHAT DETERMINES THE VALUE OF YOUR BUSINESS?

Many entrepreneurs assume their business is worth a standard EBITDA multiple—but that's just the starting point.

To maximize your exit value, you need:

1. Three years of strong financials—consistent revenue and profit growth
2. A leadership team that can run the business without you
3. Streamlined processes and efficient operations
4. Brand strength and customer loyalty
5. A lean management structure with clear growth potential

A buyer isn't just purchasing your current revenue; they're buying predictability, stability, and future profitability. A simple way to look at it is if the investor purchases the company for XX dollars, what is the annual rate of return from the net profits each year?

Will it be better than investing in the stock market? If the ROI is less than the average stock market returns, the multiples go down.

YOUR VALUE IS MORE THAN JUST NUMBERS

At the start of my career, I often compared my salary to others in my field and in other professions. It didn't take long to see the disparities. Then came the financial crisis, and my small 401(k) took a hit I didn't know how to fix. I didn't have a financial background, so I didn't know where to turn. What frustrated me most wasn't just the loss; it was the fact that someone else seemed to control my value. My career progression felt arbitrary, decided by others behind closed doors. That's when I began asking the bigger questions. How do I take ownership of my future? How do I define my own value?

That's when the idea of owning my own business took hold. It wasn't just about making more money; it was about taking control of my destiny. I had no idea how hard it would be. But I also didn't know how fulfilling it would become. Looking back now, I see the turning point clearly: It began with a decision to define my own worth and build something on my terms.

If you're thinking about selling your business one day, one of the smartest things you can do—well before that day comes—is to create a personal net worth statement. It's not just a financial document; it's a powerful tool for clarity and confidence. Here's why it matters:

- You'll need it to secure financing—lines of credit, equipment purchases, or strategic investments.
- It forces you to take a hard look at what your business is actually worth.

- It helps you prepare to negotiate from a position of strength when the time comes to sell.

Your CPA might give you a ballpark figure, but unless they specialize in valuations, it probably won't tell the whole story. Even a rough estimate, based on smart assumptions, is better than guessing. And if your business is bringing in $2 million to $3 million in annual revenue, start talking to experts now. Early insight gives you more time to plan, pivot, and grow with purpose.

THE ROLE OF TIMING AND MARKET CONDITIONS

The price you receive isn't just about your company; it's about:

1. Interest rates and tax laws
2. Stock market trends and private equity appetite
3. Your industry's short-term outlook

I wish I had studied M&A trends earlier. We did well, but with a growth and exit consultant two years prior, we could have:

- Increased our valuation
- Refined our exit strategy
- Made the transition even smoother

THIS TAX STRUCTURE SAVED US HUNDREDS OF THOUSANDS

When you're young and benefiting from the public services your taxes help fund—not to mention getting a refund when you've overpaid—you don't give it much thought. But when your tax bill starts landing in the six- or seven-figure range, you start paying very close attention to how that liability is managed. I remember reading about the trust structures that Phil Knight and other ultra-wealthy individuals had put in place.

It seemed like another world—something reserved for billionaires.

I never imagined I'd one day be exploring similar strategies to protect and preserve wealth for my family.

Every new chapter of this journey teaches you something valuable. And along the way, you meet people with deep, specialized expertise who can guide you through complex decisions. I've been incredibly fortunate in that regard.

Time and again, the right person has shown up at exactly the right moment—offering clarity, direction, or simply the wisdom I didn't yet have. Looking back, it feels like more than a coincidence. It feels like a quiet kind of grace that shaped the road ahead.

One of the smartest decisions we made was hiring a top-tier tax attorney.

A well-structured deal can save you millions in taxes, ensuring that more of your hard-earned wealth stays in your pocket.

We created:

1. Complex trust structures (dynasty trust, holding company, etc.)
2. Tax-efficient wealth transfer plans
3. A financial framework to protect multi-generational wealth

If you're planning to exit at seven, eight, or nine figures, investing in a strong tax strategy is non-negotiable.

WHAT NO ONE TELLS YOU ABOUT POST-SALE LIFE

Exiting a business is deeply personal. No two entrepreneurs walk the same path, yet those who do it right share common elements: preparation, strategy, and foresight.

If you're thinking about selling your company—or even if you're just starting out—know this: No one is ever fully prepared for an exit. There will always be unexpected twists, decisions you wish you'd made sooner, and lessons that only hindsight reveals.

However, with the right plan, the right team, and the right mindset, you can exit on your terms and walk away with the wealth you deserve.

Selling isn't just a financial transaction; it's a cultural and operational shift.

Like I said, it can be bumpy.

We were acquired by a company that had purchased multiple firms before us. We expected a smooth integration.

We were wrong. Even though it is a large international company, every office operates as an independent small business, which is not that uncommon in the professional services industry. That is a systemic problem in the industry, but that is a topic for a separate book.

The acquisitions team was impressed by our culture and business processes during the due diligence process. But after the deal was closed, we were working with the operations team, which wasn't interested in changing their ways of doing business.

I don't blame them, as it would have made their lives difficult, but had we known that upfront, we would have made a different decision or at least prepared our team better for the changes. For many employees who took pride in the processes and culture we had built, that felt like a betrayal and led to a loss of trust.

Some of our non-technical team members could not find a good fit in the new company, which again was set in its ways and not open to adapting. The leaders did not handle the emotional part of explaining that either.

This caused much disappointment, and key staff left within two years. I don't think the existing operations leaders were trying to be difficult; they just never appreciated the value of what we had built and never understood the extent of the disappointment our staff felt.

Lesson: If it's not in the contract, it doesn't count.

Unless both firms have the same work processes and culture, prepare your team for major changes—even if they promise otherwise.

The M&A team—the people you negotiate with—are not the ones who run operations. Once the sale is final, you're dealing with a new leadership team that wasn't part of those early conversations.

Include them in the early conversations and be transparent about the changes, or you will lose the magic that made you so valuable in the first place.

THE REALITY OF MERGERS AND PRIVATE EQUITY SALES

Most private equity firms exit within three to five years. If a PE firm buys your company, you should expect:

- A future resale of your business
- Structural changes to maximize investor returns
- A focus on numbers—often at the cost of culture

If they're expanding into your region or industry, your valuation might be higher. If you're just another acquisition, expect integration into their existing systems.

For key staff, there's often:

- Retention bonuses - To keep middle management during transition.
- Earn-out agreements - Owners must stay two to three years post-sale.
- Leadership restructuring - Some leaders will leave, and others will step up.

FINDING PURPOSE BEYOND YOUR EXIT

The word "retirement" comes from the French, meaning "act of retreating" or "withdrawing into seclusion." But most business owners who sell aren't looking to disappear; they're simply ready to step away from day-to-day management. What they want is meaningful engagement, not isolation. Some stay involved with the company they sold—either as part of the deal or by choice. Others turn to nonprofit work, mentoring, or community leadership. And a few are not quite done building, so they launch something new.

Even those who "retire" often dive into family time, travel, and long-postponed passions. For Asawari—my wife, business partner, and fellow adventurer—this chapter is about personal wellness, family, and rediscovering things she had to set aside while we were running the company.

As for me, I'm finishing this book, launching the Business Millionaire Club, and starting TiMoLi Foods—a new food venture built around a beloved family hot sauce recipe. After two years supporting the business transition post-sale, we're both moving forward into new work, new energy, and new purpose. This isn't retreat; it's a redefinition.

One of the biggest challenges for founders is losing authority.

As an owner, you make the decisions. After selling, you don't.

In large corporations, survival often matters more than innovation. Employees, even executives, are often focused on keeping their jobs, not taking risks.

This was a huge cultural shift for me. In a small company, everyone works toward making the company succeed. In a large company, people play not to lose.

I had to decide: continue making small changes or build my legacy?

BUILDING MY NEXT CHAPTER: HELPING OTHERS EXIT RIGHT

Selling my business was a turning point. I could have stayed, worked within the system, and made incremental improvements. I thought I would enjoy that, but as a high-drive individual, I need to push harder and achieve more than what I was getting as an employee in a large organization. I had a prominent position as the global service line leader for codes and performance-based design, but accepting incremental change does not fit my personality. In the end, I chose freedom and new adventures.

I miss interacting with some outstanding individuals I had the privilege to work with every day. In two years, I had built close friendships that I am leaving behind as I chart a new path. I enjoyed not being an owner for two years. Not having the weight of the people, projects, and profits on my shoulders was quite nice and enjoyable, but I am ready to build a new legacy and make a bigger impact.

Now, I'm helping other entrepreneurs grow and exit their businesses profitably.

THE ALL-TOO-COMMON FOUNDERS FOLLIES

They spend years building a great company, but fail to plan the sale.

They know how to sell their services but not how to sell their business.

They leave millions on the table because they don't know their true value.

Through the Business Millionaire Club, I'm combining my entrepreneurial experience, M&A knowledge, financial expertise, and negotiation skills to help business owners exit the right way.

YOUR EXIT, YOUR LEGACY

Your business is an asset—not just a job.

If you follow what I've shared in this book, you'll be in the driver's seat when it's time to sell.

The keys:

Differentiate your company.
Communicate your value.
Find the right buyer.
Negotiate from strength.

A great business deserves a great exit. Plan it well, and you'll leave wealthy, fulfilled, and ready for your next adventure.

EXITING IS A JOURNEY, NOT A CHECKLIST

A great business deserves more than just a clean break; it deserves a great exit—one that leaves you wealthy, fulfilled, and ready for whatever comes next.

Selling Code Unlimited when we did was one of the best decisions we ever made. It gave us choices we hadn't even considered. It marked the end of a powerful chapter and opened the door to the next. What I didn't fully realize, until after the sale, was just how much weight I'd been carrying—not just for the business itself but for our team, our clients, and everyone who relied on us.

Looking back, I wish we'd had someone like me in our corner. Sure, we figured out the technical parts of the exit. We read books, studied the financials, and brought in experts to help with the legal and tax details. However, what we didn't find—at least not easily—was someone who could speak to the bigger picture: the emotional side, the identity shift, and the complexity of stepping away from something you built from the ground up.

That's the lesson. Start planning early. Update your plan often. Above all, I would work with a consultant who sees the full picture—someone who understands both the hard numbers and the human experience. Because your exit isn't just a transaction, it's a transformation.

√ Eighty percent of most small business owners' net worth is their business. Yet 70% don't know how to monetize. Avoid the pitfalls while moving toward profit (and purpose) at mybizmc.com/book.

KEY #8: THE HEARTBEAT OF AN EXIT: COMMUNICATING WITH YOUR PEOPLE AND MANAGING THEIR EXPECTATIONS

Selling your business isn't just a financial event.

It's an emotional earthquake.

It stirs up fear, excitement, uncertainty, grief, and hope—sometimes all in the same meeting. And while you might be focused on the numbers, the contracts, and the handshakes, your team is wondering: *What does this mean for me?*

Here's the hard truth: You can have the cleanest books, the strongest EBITDA, and the smoothest legal docs—and still blow the deal if you mishandle the human side.

Because no matter how much logic you bring to the table, emotions always ride shotgun. And if you're not ready for them, they'll take the wheel.

This chapter is about preparing for that ride.

It's about how to lead your team through the exit with clarity, courage, and compassion.

How to address the fears they won't say out loud.

How to calm the storm before it begins.

And how to walk through one of the most complex moments of your career with your values intact and your people (mostly) on board.

To be honest, I didn't get it all right.

I underestimated how intense it would be.

I made some mistakes and learned a lot.

Some staff panicked.

Some left.

Some lashed out.

And a few quietly doubted my integrity.

In our case, despite the challenges, in the end, many stayed. And more than one came back later to say, "Now I see what you built and how much you cared."

You can't control everyone's reaction. But you can control how you show up.

In the pages that follow, I'll walk you through:

1. The psychology of your team during a sale
2. How to prepare people early (even before you think they need to know)
3. Why fear spreads faster than facts and how to contain it
4. What to say (and not say) when change is coming
5. How to honor your culture even as you hand off your company

If you've built something worth buying, chances are it's because of the people who helped you build it. Honor that. Respect that. And lead like it matters.

Because it does.

Let's begin.

PREPARING YOUR PEOPLE: THE MOST OVERLOOKED (AND MOST CRITICAL) PART OF THE SALE

When most business owners think about selling, their minds jump to numbers, legal contracts, and deal structures. And yes—those are important.

However, there's another part of the process that's just as crucial, often harder to navigate, and capable of sinking the deal if mishandled: the emotions—yours, your staff's, and the buyer's. Especially your staffs.

Because when you announce that you're selling your company—the company your team has worked hard to build, day after day—it's more than just business. It's deeply personal. It's unsettling. It can feel like betrayal to some and a golden opportunity to others.

And if you don't handle it well, it can spark chaos—fear, frustration, resistance, and even sabotage.

So how do you lead through that storm?

You prepare early. You communicate clearly. And you lead with empathy.

Here's how:

1. Share the "why" early and often.
2. Don't wait until the paperwork is signed. As soon as you're considering a sale, start crafting your message. Your team needs to hear why this is happening—and more importantly—what's in it for them.
3. Anticipate fear, don't avoid it.

Many employees will hear "sale" or "merger" and immediately assume layoffs, chaos, or culture collapse. After all, that's the narrative they see in the news. But those headlines mostly come from product companies—where roles get duplicated and departments get merged. Service businesses are different. Talent is the product. And smart buyers know that.

Recognize that every person will react differently.

Not everyone joined your firm for the same reason. Not everyone has the same vision for their future. Some will be excited. Some will panic. Others will just be confused. That's normal. Don't try to please everyone. Focus on managing the range of reactions, especially from key influencers inside the company.

Keep an eye on the fence-sitters and the pot-stirrers.

In every organization, there are people who quietly influence many others. If they're anxious, skeptical, or misinformed, they can derail morale—or even scare off a buyer. Talk to them directly. Hear their concerns. Give them reasons to believe in the transition.

Be honest but not overly detailed.

There will be parts of the deal you can't share. And some aspects that won't feel favorable to everyone. Let your team know that. Set expectations. Reinforce what you can promise: stability, opportunity, and thoughtful leadership through the change.

I'll be honest with you: This part of the journey surprised me.

I underestimated how intense the emotional responses would be. Some team members panicked. Others lashed out. One even had a meltdown that almost spooked the buyer.

Some expected to be rewarded like owners, even though they never took on the risks or responsibilities that ownership requires. Others assumed that everyone would be laid off because that's what happens in the movies. But in our case—as a service-based firm—that couldn't be further from the truth.

Still, fear doesn't ask for facts. Fear operates on stories. Your job is to rewrite those stories before they take root.

Some people say, "The sunrise is worth the storm."

You can't predict the future, and you can't control the present—but you can prepare. You can stay steady in uncertain times and help guide those around you so that, together, you all make it through the storm. Leadership in business—and in life—isn't about avoiding the waves. It's about steering through them with clarity, strength, and intention. Because no matter how rough it gets, the sun always rises. And after the storm, that sunrise feels especially beautiful.

WHAT ACTUALLY HAPPENS POST-SALE?

There's no single typical post-sale experience. Every business and every transition is unique.

As I spoke with dozens of firm owners while researching this book and building my exit consulting practice, one theme came up repeatedly.

"I wish we'd started sooner. I wish we'd prepared better for the fact that one day, we'd exit."

That regret is universal.

Because no matter how different the business or the deal, one truth remains: Your future buyer is coming. The question is whether you'll be ready.

Prepare early. Plan well. So, when it's time to let go, you don't just walk away; you cash out with confidence, leaving a business built to last.

In many acquisitions—especially in service firms—there is no massive layoff. In fact, the acquiring company often wants to keep the team intact. Sometimes, team members are asked to resign and be rehired under the new entity. This allows salaries to be adjusted to the market, roles to be aligned, and everyone to start with a clean slate.

Often, compensation goes up. Sometimes, roles get more focused. And in many cases, nothing changes at all for the first year or two, allowing time for everyone to adjust.

But all of that only works if your people stay.
And people stay when they feel:

- Respected
- Informed
- Seen and heard
- Part of something bigger than themselves

Instead of Layoffs

Our team didn't see the sale coming. We didn't plan it far in advance. But after COVID turned the world upside down, we realized we needed a long-term strategy.

Construction halted. Projects paused. Uncertainty ruled. We had to pivot, not reactively but strategically.

Instead of layoffs, we cut senior salaries. My wife and I reduced our pay by 75%. Junior staff took small, rotating reductions. We applied for (and received) a PPP loan that helped us keep everyone on payroll. We weathered the storm better than most.

However, looking back, I don't think our team fully realized how carefully we navigated that storm. That's not their fault. We chose not to share all the behind-the-scenes decisions. We protected them from the worry because that's what leaders do.

Later, when we did sell the company, some staff told us how much they valued our culture—especially after seeing how things worked elsewhere. That felt good. It was the kind of delayed compliment that meant the world.

Still, had they understood our values and decisions earlier, maybe the transition would've been smoother for them. Maybe they would've had more peace along the way.

FINAL THOUGHTS

If you're planning to sell, don't just prep your books and tidy up your contracts.

Prepare your people.

Because a business isn't a product on a shelf, it's a living, breathing ecosystem. And when you sell it, you're not just selling assets; you're passing on a culture, a team, and a legacy.

That legacy starts with how you lead through the emotional rollercoaster of transition.

Talk early.

Share your why.

Listen with patience.

Accept that not everyone will stay—and that's okay.

Help those who stay feel proud to be part of what comes next.

Because the goal isn't just to exit with a big check.

The goal is to exit with your values intact, your relationships strong, and your legacy respected.

And yes, if you do it right, you can walk away a millionaire.

However, more importantly, you can walk away knowing you built something worth buying, worth believing in, and worth remembering.

KEY #9: THE TRIGGER TIMING: EXIT AT THE RIGHT MOMENT

Timing shouldn't rely on luck; developing a clear strategy allows you to recognize when the conditions are primed for maximum value. Even though you cannot time the market, when the market is hot everything seems to work great. Like stocks, business valuations fluctuate. Know when the market is ripe for your exit and be ready to seize the moment.

In business, as in life, timing is everything; it is taking advantage of the circumstances. It overcomes all mistakes and missteps. You wouldn't harvest crops before they're ripe, and you wouldn't sell a stock just because the market feels "okay." The same principle applies to exiting your business. A great exit isn't just about preparation; it's about recognizing the right moment to step away and maximize value.

However, timing is part luck and part strategy. Market conditions, industry trends, buyer interest, and economic cycles all can change for the better or worse and affect the value of your business. The key is knowing how to read those signals and act with confidence when the stars align.

In this chapter, we'll explore how to identify your perfect exit window, anticipate market shifts, and plan with precision.

Because when you get the timing right, your exit won't just be profitable; it will be transformative.

Let's uncover the timing trigger and make sure you're ready to pull it when the moment arrives.

SEIZING THE MOMENT

Looking back, there were key moments when I chose to seize an opportunity—and those decisions changed the entire trajectory of my life.

It's a mindset: the willingness to leap into something new without letting fear of failure hold you back. Part of it came naturally, but I worked hard to sharpen it over time.

Sure, there are people who stay in their lanes and still reach the top. Others avoid risk and somehow hit their goals anyway. But if we're honest, each of us can name a handful of moments when saying yes changed everything.

For me, those moments included:

- Accepting my first client while still in third-year architecture
- Choosing the University of Oregon
- Working the graveyard shift at EMU
- Taking the leap to become a code consultant
- Starting Code Unlimited
- Ultimately, deciding to sell

Each choice wasn't just a step forward; it was a pivot that opened new possibilities.

That's the truth about building and selling a business for real wealth:

1. You don't get there by standing still
2. You get there by saying yes when it matters most

3. You get there by seeing opportunity in places others see risk

Because in the end, those bold decisions don't just build a business.

They build the life you really want.

There is a right time to exit, look for that, and plan well. Like the stock market and individual company stock, the valuations of private companies are swayed by the amount of money in the market and the need for your kind of company to attract multiple potential buyers.

SELLING YOUR BUSINESS: WHY TIMING THE MARKET IS A MYTH AND WHAT TO DO INSTEAD

If you've ever invested in stocks or built a retirement portfolio, you've likely heard the golden rule: Don't try to time the market. Instead, steady, strategic investing over time yields better results than chasing quick wins.

Selling your business follows the same principle.

Many entrepreneurs dream of selling at the perfect moment—buy low, sell high—but market conditions, buyer interest, and economic shifts don't wait for your timeline. The price you get for your company depends on factors beyond your control, from industry trends to tax laws, interest rates, and even geopolitical events.

Waiting for the "perfect" time can backfire. If you're not prepared, you may end up selling under pressure—or missing the best opportunity altogether. The key is to prepare early, build strategically, and align your business for a high-value exit—whenever the right moment arrives.

Samir Mokashi, CEPA® M.Arch. Ar.

How to Maximize Your Business's Value Before Selling

A successful sale doesn't happen overnight. It's a process, not an event. The best exits are planned two to three years in advance to ensure your business is attractive, resilient, and built to thrive without you.

Here's how to position your company for a high-value exit:

- Build a business that buyers want.
- Make it resilient - A company that runs smoothly without you commands a higher price. If your success depends on one person or a small team, buyers will hesitate.
- Create strong processes - Scalable, repeatable systems increase predictability and make your business more valuable.
- Develop recurring revenue - Buyers love consistent, predictable cash flow. Subscription models, contracts, and long-term customer relationships increase valuation.
- Invest in a top-tier team - A well-trained, committed leadership team makes your business more transferable.

Identify Potential Buyers Early

Who would benefit most from acquiring your company? Competitors? Strategic partners? Private equity firms? The earlier you build relationships, the more leverage you'll have.

Work with an experienced M&A advisor. They maintain deep connections with potential buyers and can bring serious offers to the table—often faster than you can on your own.

Diversify your exit options. If the perfect buyer doesn't appear, will you be forced to sell under duress? Consider alternative paths like mergers, roll-ups, or internal transitions.

144

Prepare for Wealth Management and Post-Sale Planning

Years ago, I read *Rich Dad Poor Dad* by Robert Kiyosaki, and it changed the way I saw everything.

Most people work endlessly for a paycheck just to cover their needs. But the smart ones make their money work for them—even while they sleep.

Early in my career, no matter how much I earned, I was haunted by the same worries:

- Rising cost of living
- Market crashes
- Unpredictable global events that could wreck my plans

I wanted freedom from that fear. That's why I chose to build a business instead of just collecting a salary. I wanted something I controlled—an asset that could grow beyond my time and effort.

That shift in thinking didn't stop there. It made me get serious about investing. I taught myself the game and got pretty good at it—but I realized something crucial: I didn't have the time or resources to manage it all on my own.

So, I chose a better path. I brought in experts to help me protect and grow my wealth.

Because if you want lasting freedom—the kind that lets you sell your business for millions and truly enjoy it—you have to think bigger:

1. Build assets, not just income
2. Invest wisely and intentionally
3. Surround yourself with people who know how to make your money work harder than you do

That's how you stop trading time for money. That's how you create a legacy that outlives you.

- Protect your wealth - Selling your business isn't just about getting a high price; it's about keeping what you earn. Work with a tax strategist and investment manager to safeguard your financial future.
- Establish trusts and tax-efficient strategies - A poorly planned sale can result in huge tax liabilities. Start structuring your wealth plan long before closing the deal.
- Reinvest wisely - Once you exit, how will you grow your capital? A down market could mean reinvesting at a discount—even if you don't get top dollar for your business.

THE BIGGEST MISTAKES TO AVOID

Many business owners wait too long to think about selling— often until they're forced into it. Here's what not to do:

- Waiting until the last minute - A rushed sale rarely delivers maximum value. Start positioning your business now—before you need to sell.
- Ignoring market conditions - Timing may be unpredictable, but being aware of trends helps you act at the right moment.
- Assuming buyers will magically appear: -They won't. You need a strategy to attract and engage them.
- Failing to prepare for life after the sale - What comes next? A new venture? Consulting? Philanthropy? Clarity on your next chapter reduces uncertainty and regret.

LESSONS FROM MY EXIT

When I sold my business, I had a few companies in mind as potential buyers, but I didn't build relationships with them early enough. Had I done so, I would have had more negotiating power and flexibility.

Ultimately, I did well. But looking back, I was more lucky than strategic.

I'm writing this book so you don't have to rely on luck. With the right preparation, you can exit on your terms at the right time for the best price.

Your business has been your life's work—now, make sure your exit is just as intentional.

KEY #10: THE STEWARD'S MINDSET: PASSING THE TORCH, PROTECTING THE LEGACY

S elling your business is not the end of the journey. It's the beginning of a new kind of leadership.

You've poured years—maybe decades—into building something real. Not just a company but a community. Not just profits but trust. You've created systems, mentored people, and solved problems no one else saw coming. And now, as you prepare to hand it over, the question isn't just how much you will make; the real question is what you will leave behind.

This chapter is about legacy. It's about influence that lasts beyond ownership. It's about stepping into the next phase of your role—not as CEO but as steward, guide, and mentor. Because once the ink is dry and the business is officially in someone else's hands, you still have something priceless to offer: wisdom, relationships, and a deep understanding of what made your business work.

Most acquiring companies underestimate that value. They see revenue, assets, and operations—but they miss the culture, the trust, and the human glue that holds it all together. That's why many mergers stumble. They forget that goodwill isn't automatic. It must be earned, protected, and passed down with care.

In this chapter, you'll learn how to prepare your team, your clients, and yourself for this pivotal transition. You'll see how to:

1. Shift from day-to-day leader to trusted mentor
2. Ensure your company's strengths are integrated—not erased
3. Align cultures so the acquisition feels like a shared future, not a takeover
4. Negotiate your influence into the deal, so your voice continues to shape what you built

The exit is a moment. The legacy is what follows.
Done right, you won't just sell a business.
You'll pass the torch—and watch the fire grow.

HANDING OVER A LEGACY

From day one at Code Unlimited, we knew the day would come when someone else would own it or lead it. That was always part of the plan.

However, no matter how strategic you are, you can't ignore the emotions tied to the journey—and to the people who travel it with you.

As you prepare to scale and eventually exit, remember:

- Your team isn't just executing tasks; they're sharing your vision
- Your customers aren't just buying services; they're buying trust
- You're not just building value on paper; you're building relationships that define your legacy

You can plan every detail of your sale. You can optimize for the highest price. But when you look back, you'll realize the real impact wasn't just financial.

It was personal. And that's something you can't afford to forget.

When you sell your business, you are not just walking away; you are handing over a legacy.

For years, you've been the leader, the decision-maker, the person responsible for the success of your employees and the growth of the company. Your hard work has built not just a business but goodwill, influence, and a reputation that extends far beyond the balance sheet.

However, after the sale, your role changes. You are no longer the owner. You are no longer the authority figure at the top of the hierarchy. The question is: How do you transition from leader to mentor while ensuring your legacy thrives?

THE POWER OF INFLUENCE BEYOND OWNERSHIP

Your leadership didn't come from a title; it came from:

- Your ability to inspire others
- Your experience, wisdom, and strategic thinking
- The trust and goodwill you built with your team and clients

After an acquisition, it can be challenging for employees—who are used to seeing you as the ultimate decision-maker—to accept you in a new role. If you prepare them well, they will understand that your real power wasn't in ownership but in leadership.

The most effective way to transition post-merger is to become a mentor.

Guide key employees as they step into leadership roles.

Help clients feel confident in the new company structure. Pass down insights and industry knowledge that took you years to gain.

A strong mentor ensures that the business doesn't just survive the transition; it thrives.

Why Many Mergers Fail to Leverage Goodwill

Not all acquiring companies know how to handle the transition well.

Some see an acquisition as just a financial transaction; others focus too much on the operations, while others focus on the culture. An acquisition is made up of all of these and some more. It is way more than revenue and assets. It is imperative to truly understand the people, relationships, and expertise that made the company successful.

Common mistakes acquiring companies make include:

- Treating the acquired business as a commodity - Assuming that success will continue without investing in culture, leadership, or customer relationships
- Overwriting the acquired company's strengths - Pushing rigid systems that don't integrate the unique strengths of the acquired firm
- Failing to transition leadership properly - Assuming that new leadership will automatically gain the trust and respect of employees and clients

The result is lost customers, disengaged employees, and struggling integration.

The best mergers are the ones where the acquired company plays a proactive role in shaping the transition.

How to Ensure a Smooth Transition

Change is the only guarantee in business—and in life.

Yet we always hope the next transition will be easy—smooth waters, clear skies, no surprises.

But let's be honest, that's rarely how it goes.

Whether you're selling your business, merging with another, or handing the reins to someone new, you'll face unpredictable conditions:

- Times when the wind dies completely, leaving you stuck in the doldrums—no momentum, no clear path forward
- Times when headwinds push hard against your plans, testing your resolve
- And yes, moments of glorious tailwinds that make everything faster and easier—if you're prepared to harness them

The difference between a disastrous voyage and a successful one isn't the weather. It's the captain.

You need leadership that's calm in crisis, adaptable when the winds shift, and experienced enough to see what's coming over the horizon.

If you want to make your next big move successful—especially your exit—you need to:

1. Acknowledge that change will be messy and plan for it
2. Invest in steady, seasoned leadership—yours or someone else's
3. Communicate with your crew so they're ready for whatever comes
4. Chart your course carefully, but stay nimble enough to adjust

Because when you're selling your business, you're not just transferring assets.

You're handing over a ship.

And the smoother the journey you promise, the higher the price someone will pay to take the helm.

If you want your company's legacy, culture, and strengths to survive post-sale, you must plan before the deal is signed.

Here are four steps to make it happen:

1. Make Leadership Transition a Priority

   - Talk openly about the new roles and titles and reporting structures
   - Communicate your mentorship role to employees and clients
   - Help establish a leadership pipeline between the buyer and seller teams before you leave

2. Protect Your Business's Strengths

   - Highlight the core competencies that made your business successful
   - Work with the acquiring company to integrate strengths, not erase them
   - Push for a structured and transparent transition plan as part of the merger agreement

3. Use Your Influence to Align Cultures

   - Help everyone understand why the business was bought
   - Help bridge the gap between the two cultures
   - Educate new leadership on why your company succeeded and how to preserve those strengths

4. Negotiate for Influence in the Legal Agreement

- Don't assume the new owners will naturally maintain your company's strengths
- Make it part of the deal—include leadership transition, culture integration, and customer relationship management in the agreement
- Ensure the integration strategy benefits both sides—not just the acquiring company

THE LEGACY YOU LEAVE BEHIND

A well-managed transition doesn't just protect your business; it enhances its value.

Employees step into leadership roles with confidence.

Clients feel secure and supported through the transition.

The acquiring company gains not just a business but a high-performing, engaged team.

If done right, your influence extends beyond ownership—shaping the company's future, strengthening your industry reputation, and ensuring your years of effort leave a lasting impact.

Plan ahead. Protect your legacy. Pass the torch with purpose.

Don't Forget!

A business is like a ship, and titles are the compass. Without clear roles and responsibilities, even the best crew can drift off course. I've seen companies where no one knows who does what, and others where inflated titles sound impressive but mean nothing.

When you're preparing to sell, clarity matters more than ever. Buyers look past the job titles and into your structure. They want to know who makes decisions, how your team functions, and whether the company can run without you.

When roles are clear, your business runs better, sells for more, and continues to thrive long after you've stepped away.

I've seen it all: companies where everyone has a bland, forgettable title and others where junior hires walk around with grandiose labels that look good on LinkedIn but mean nothing on the org chart.

A fancy title might impress friends and family, but it doesn't build a business that lasts.

What truly matters to your team and your future buyer is clarity.

Titles only have real value when they define clear roles, responsibilities, and pathways for growth. When titles are well-defined, they're more than labels. They become sign-posts for:

- What a person is accountable for
- How decisions get made
- How careers advance within your company

This is even more critical when you're preparing for a sale or acquisition.

Why? Because titles, roles, and reporting lines aren't just organizational details. They're emotional territory. They carry personal significance, pride, and sometimes even fear.

When companies merge, these attachments can become baggage:

- Confusion over who does what
- Turf wars over influence
- Resentment about perceived demotions or loss of status

If you want a smooth, lucrative exit, you can't ignore this.

Here's how to get it right:

1. Define roles and titles with crystal clarity—no fluff, no ambiguity
2. Align titles with real authority and decision-making power
3. Create clear paths for career progression that motivate your team
4. Communicate openly about any changes, so people feel respected and heard

Because at the end of the day, buyers don't just invest in your financials.

They invest in your people—and in the structure that lets them do their best work.

Get this right, and you won't just sell your business for more.

You'll hand over something truly built to last.

Post-exit roles, responsibilities, culture evolution, and incentives for your key players aren't just footnotes; they're the lifeblood of a smooth transition. A seamless transition isn't just about contracts.

Every business is built on people—relationships, trust, and shared purpose. Yet, when it comes to exit planning, the human factor is often treated as an afterthought, tucked into the fine print of legal agreements. But here's the truth: The people side of your exit isn't a detail; it's the lifeblood of a smooth transition.

Successful exit planning will include a clear articulation of:

1. Owners' role/responsibility post transition and eventual exit/retirement
2. Roles and responsibilities for key employees post transition

3. The change or evolution of the company culture

Negotiate a severance package or retention bonus for those who stay and those who leave within a certain period.

Imagine building a bridge to your next chapter, only to realize the pillars holding it up—your team, your culture, your key players—were left unsteady. Without clarity on post-exit roles, responsibilities, and incentives, even the most promising deals can unravel.

Next, we'll explore how to plan for your team's future, define roles with precision, and create incentives that keep your best people motivated through and beyond the transition. When you honor the people who've helped build your success, you don't just hand over a business; you pass on a thriving legacy. Let's get it right.

Leading Through a Merger or Acquisition

Leading your team through a merger or acquisition is like steering a ship through fog. The destination is promising, but visibility drops fast.

Roles blur. Authority gets fuzzy.

During negotiations, everyone is polite, plays nice, and is careful not to reveal too much. But behind the smiles? Hesitation. Unspoken fears. People hold their cards close, afraid of losing influence or security.

This creates a breeding ground for:

- Ambiguity
- Misunderstandings
- Distrust that can derail the deal

Some confusion is inevitable. You're blending two worlds. But most of the chaos is avoidable.

It all comes down to leadership and open communication.

When you lead decisively and communicate clearly, you give your team the confidence to move forward together. You replace fear with alignment. You turn uncertainty into momentum.

To navigate this successfully:

1. Set crystal-clear expectations about roles and decision-making
2. Foster honest conversations—no hidden agendas
3. Address fears head-on, so your people feel heard and valued
4. Model calm, confident leadership that inspires trust

Because if you want your business to sell for top dollar—and thrive under new ownership—you can't just manage the numbers.

You must manage the people.

Do that well, and you don't just close a deal. You build a legacy.

First, acknowledge their concerns. Your team wants stability, and the past cannot be restored. Instead, offer a clear, forward-looking vision that reassures them of their place in the new structure.

Uncertainty breeds fear. Transparent and frequent communication will be your greatest tool in calming anxieties and aligning expectations.

Those who embrace change will thrive. Those who resist may choose to leave. Your job as a leader is to guide both groups with wisdom and integrity.

Give employees a structured way to see themselves in the company's future. Without it, they will make assumptions—often negative or misguided.

HELP YOUR PEOPLE DEFINE SUCCESS IN THEIR NEW LANDSCAPE

Here's how:

1. Provide a roadmap - What will success look like one, two, or three years from now?
2. Encourage conversations around career growth, stability, and opportunities within the merged organization.
3. Offer mentorship and guidance for those seeking new roles, whether inside or outside the company.
4. Define roles and responsibilities early before uncertainty erodes trust.
5. Balance technical qualifications (education, licenses, certifications) with leadership qualities, communication skills, and adaptability.
6. Organize listening sessions to gather insights on what employees envision for a successful transition. Frame the conversation positively: "What would a thriving merger look like?" rather than focusing on potential problems.
7. Prepare for the unexpected.

Even the best-laid plans can be disrupted by external factors—market shifts, economic downturns, policy changes. Build contingency plans (Plan B and Plan C) to keep your business resilient.

Many employees don't see how global trends impact their daily work. As a leader, it's your role to connect those dots and prepare them for shifting dynamics.

BUILDING A STRONGER CULTURE POST-MERGER

When a business gets acquired, everyone's eyes lock onto the numbers—revenue, profit margins, and performance charts.

But here's the truth most people don't want to talk about:

Culture doesn't wait patiently in the corner. It either fuels your success or poisons it.

Too often, leaders shove the emotional impact of a merger under the rug—hurt feelings, confusion, resentment—thinking these "soft" issues will work themselves out.

They don't.

As Peter Drucker famously said, "Culture eats strategy for breakfast."

And if you ignore it, culture will eat your financial results for lunch—and dinner, too.

When cultural integration is neglected, you risk:

- A team divided by mistrust and hidden agendas
- Slower performance, lower morale, and higher turnover
- Lost momentum right when you need it most

But when you make culture a priority, you unlock:

1. A unified team inspired to deliver extraordinary results
2. Smoother transitions that protect—and often grow—profit
3. A strong, resilient company that buyers are eager to invest in

If you want your exit to be more than a short-lived pay-day—if you want it to be a legacy—then remember: Culture isn't a box you tick after the deal closes. It's the invisible force that determines whether your million-dollar dream thrives or dies.

A merger doesn't have to mean losing the tight-knit culture that made your company special. However, maintaining that sense of connection within a larger organization requires intentional effort.

Avoid the "assembly line" mentality. Some corporations treat employees like cogs in a machine, stripping away autonomy and creativity. That approach fails in knowledge-based industries like law, architecture, and engineering, where expertise and collaboration are key.

Embrace the "production line" model. Unlike an assembly line, a well-run production line values teamwork, individual contribution, and efficiency. It strikes a balance, leveraging collective strengths while maintaining high-quality, personalized service.

The most successful transitions happen when leaders recognize that people—not just processes—drive value. By prioritizing communication, offering a clear vision, and fostering a culture of collaboration, you ensure that your exit is not just financially successful but also leaves a lasting, positive legacy.

Not everyone will stay—but if you lead with integrity, even those who leave will remain goodwill ambassadors for your business. And that, in the end, is a true measure of leadership.

√ Eighty percent of most small business owners' net worth is their business. Yet 70% don't know how to monetize. Avoid the pitfalls while moving toward profit (and purpose) at mybizmc.com/book.

THE EXIT IS JUST
THE BEGINNING

If you've made it this far, congratulations. You've already done something that most people never will; you've taken the time to look at your business, your mindset, and your future with the end in mind. You've stepped out of the daily grind long enough to think strategically, to see the bigger picture, and to imagine what it will feel like to walk away not just with a handshake but with the resources, security, and freedom to design the next chapter of your life.

Exiting as a millionaire isn't about luck. It isn't about having the perfect business idea or waiting for the stars to align. It's about ordinary actions done with extraordinary consistency. It's about showing up every day with the willingness to do what most won't—digging into your numbers, building the right systems, leading with values, and never letting fear or comfort talk you into playing small.

If you take one thing from my journey, let it be this: You don't have to be extraordinary to create extraordinary results. I started without money, without connections, and without a safety net. What I did have was a willingness to learn, to adapt, to take calculated risks, and to surround myself with people who were better than I was in the areas that mattered.

I learned to trust my gut when the data was incomplete and to lean on the data when my gut was getting in the way.

You've also seen that a successful exit isn't just about the money. Yes, the payout matters. It gives you choices, protects your future, and funds the impact you want to make. However, the real win is in building something that matters. A business that outlives you. A team that continues to thrive after you've stepped away. A legacy that your clients, your employees, and your industry will remember. That's the difference between simply cashing out and truly exiting well.

Throughout this book, I've shared what worked for me, what didn't, and what I wish I'd known sooner. The strategies here aren't complicated. They're not reserved for a select few. They are the same principles that any business owner can apply if they're willing to stop treating their business like a job and start treating it like an asset. The challenge is that most people don't do it. They get caught in the comfort of the familiar or the chaos of the urgent, and they never make the moves that would change their trajectory.

You now know better. You have the map in your hands. And while the road will still throw you surprises—economic shifts, competitive pressures, personal curveballs—you'll have the tools to adapt. You'll know when to push through and when to pivot. You'll know how to protect the value you've built and how to position it so buyers see it as irresistible, not just interesting.

If you're in the middle of your journey, let this be the nudge to start thinking about your exit now. Don't wait until burnout or a crisis forces your hand. Build with the end in mind from today. Every decision you make—from who you hire to how you price to the processes you put in place—either increases or decreases your business's value in the eyes of a future buyer.

And when the day comes, make it count. Don't let all those years of work dissolve into a quiet fade-out. Walk away with your head high, your bank account full, and the knowledge that you've created something worth buying and worth remembering.

I wrote this book because I've lived both sides of the equation: the uncertainty of starting with nothing and the satisfaction of exiting with more than I dreamed possible. If my story can help you take even one step closer to your millionaire exit, the effort has been worth it.

So now it's your turn. Take the lessons, the mindset, the strategies—and act. Build your enterprise. Scale it smart. Prepare it for the right buyer. And when the moment comes, walk into your next chapter with clarity, confidence, and the resources to make the kind of impact that only comes when you've turned your business into your greatest asset.

I'll be cheering for you. And when your exit happens, let's celebrate together—with a good glass of wine, watching the sun set somewhere beautiful, knowing that you built it, you sold it, and you made it matter.

You have nurtured an innovative culture, built an impactful business, and carved a formidable legacy. Now it is time to reap the rewards of your hard work and walk away wealthy. Today is day one of that journey.

ABOUT THE AUTHOR

Samir Mokashi CEPA® M.Arch. Ar. has shared his insights on stages and in boardrooms, through technical papers and industry journals, and, now, through a book designed to help business owners transform their companies from income generators into wealth-creating assets.

Samir's story is a living example of what's possible when vision meets grit, when strategy meets heart, and when persistence refuses to quit. *The Millionaire Exit* is not just a book but the distilled wisdom of a person who started with nothing and walked away with everything he needed to live life (free on his terms), create generational wealth, and help others do the same.

Against the advice of many who warned him not to share his "trade secrets," Samir decided that helping other entrepreneurs win was worth more than holding back.

His message is simple and powerful: You don't have to be extraordinary to achieve extraordinary results. You just have to take the right actions in the right order with the right mindset.

Samir's career has never followed a straight line, and that's the point. He arrived in the United States to pursue a Master of Architecture. From there, he reinvented himself repeatedly: semiconductor FAB expert, building regulations authority, founder of multiple businesses, high-stakes project manager, business consultant, and, most recently, co-creator of a fusion sauce brand. Along the way, he became a C-suite executive, a sought-after strategist, and a mentor to entrepreneurs ready to think bigger and build smarter.

His subject matter expertise spans semiconductor FAB design, hazardous materials management, mass timber, building codes, chemical-resistant coatings, sustainable business growth, and—his specialty—positioning a business for a profitable exit. His ability to bridge technical mastery with strategic vision has made him a trusted voice in industries where precision and profitability go hand in hand.

The Millionaire Exit is his way of passing the torch—so when you sell your business, you don't just walk away with money in the bank but with a legacy worth leaving.

ACKNOWLEDGMENTS

I wish to express my deepest gratitude to my wife, Asawari, who believed in me when it was all just a dream, kept my flights of fancy grounded, maintained impeccable books, and made huge contributions to the success of the business, without ever taking any credit. She never gave up, even during the COVID years, when the future was uncertain and path increasingly difficult. To my children, who are wise beyond their years, who inspire me by their curiosity, compassion, and creativity, and fuel my drive by their unwavering support.

To all the employees of Code Unlimited, who made it a great place to work by their kindness, collaboration, innovation, inspiration, and dedication. Special thanks to Tom Jaleski, who jumped in with both feet when I pitched him the idea of Code Unlimited in the Cornelius Pass Roadhouse, joined as the first employee of Code Unlimited, and calls me a "A Force of Nature."

To my parents, siblings, in-laws, and extended family, you make me smile, believe in the goodness of the world, and remind me to be thankful. My teachers, professors, clients, and colleagues, you welcomed me with open arms, shared your insights, picked me up when I failed, gave me feedback when I needed it, provided answers to complex questions, and made me the person I am today.